D0288194

SUGAR
FREE

SUGAR FREE

The Complete Guide
to Quit Sugar
& Lose Weight Naturally

SONOMA
PRESS

Copyright © 2014 by Sonoma Press, Berkeley, California

No part of this publication may be reproduced, stored in a retrieval system or transmitted in any form or by any means, electronic, mechanical, photocopying, recording, scanning or otherwise, except as permitted under Sections 107 or 108 of the 1976 United States Copyright Act, without the prior written permission of the Publisher. Requests to the Publisher for permission should be addressed to the Permissions Department, Rockridge Press, 918 Parker St, Suite A-12, Berkeley, CA 94710.

Limit of Liability/Disclaimer of Warranty: The Publisher and the author make no representations or warranties with respect to the accuracy or completeness of the contents of this work and specifically disclaim all warranties, including without limitation warranties of fitness for a particular purpose. No warranty may be created or extended by sales or promotional materials. The advice and strategies contained herein may not be suitable for every situation. This work is sold with the understanding that the publisher is not engaged in rendering medical, legal or other professional advice or services. If professional assistance is required, the services of a competent professional person should be sought. Neither the Publisher nor the author shall be liable for damages arising herefrom. The fact that an individual, organization or website is referred to in this work as a citation and/or potential source of further information does not mean that the author or the Publisher endorses the information the individual, organization or website may provide or recommendations they/it may make. Further, readers should be aware that Internet websites listed in this work may have changed or disappeared between when this work was written and when it is read.

For general information on our other products and services or to obtain technical support, please contact our Customer Care Department within the U.S. at (866) 744-2665, or outside the U.S. at (510) 253-0500.

Sonoma Press publishes its books in a variety of electronic and print formats. Some content that appears in print may not be available in electronic books, and vice versa.

TRADEMARKS: Sonoma Press and the Sonoma Press logo are trademarks or registered trademarks of Callisto Media Inc. and/or its affiliates, in the United States and other countries, and may not be used without written permission. All other trademarks are the property of their respective owners Sonoma Press is not associated with any product or vendor mentioned in this book.

Photo Credits: Zabert Sandmann Verlag/Jan-Peter Westermann/Stockfood, pp ii-iii; Colin Cooke/Stockfood, p. vi (top left); Charles Schiller Photography/Stockfood, p. 10; Sporrer/Skowronek/Stockfood, p. 22; Westend61/Stockfood, p. 36; Valerie Janssen/Stockfood, p. 44; Veronika Studer/Stockfood, p. 63 (top right); Martin Dyrlov/Stockfood, p. 64; Samantha Linsell/Stockfood, p. 68; Dave King/Stockfood, p. 70; Yagi Studio/Media Bakery, p. 74; Tengwei Huang/Getty, p. 79; Fotosearch RM/Stockfood, p. 103; Colin Cooke/Stockfood, p. 110; Rua Castilho/Stockfood, p. 117; William Lingwood/Stockfood, p. 123; La Food-Thomas Dhellemmes/Stockfood, p. 130; ISTL/Stockfood, p. 139; Sam Stowell/Stockfood, p. 142; Rua Castilho/Stockfood, p. 146; Keller & Keller Photography/Stockfood, p. 150; ISTL/Stockfood, p. 157; Gabriel Bucataru/Stocksy, p. 163; Michael Wissing/Stockfood, p. 167; George Crudo/Stockfood, p. 171; Gareth Morgans/Stockfood, p. 174; Tanya Zouev/Stockfood, p. 181; Tina Rupp/Stockfood, p. 188; Alexandra Grablewski/Getty, p. 195; Harald Walker/Stocksy, p. 201; Westermann & Buroh Studios/Stockfood, p. 205; Rita Maas/Getty, p. 208; Richard Jung Photography/Stockfood, p. 216; Charlotte Tolhurst/Stockfood, p. 227; Dan Duchars/Stockfood, p 236; Iain Bagwell/Stockfood, p. 243; Tomasz Jakusz/Stockfood, p. 250; Brett Stevens/Media Bakery, p. 258; Tanya Zouev/Stockfood, p. 267; Stuart West/Stockfood, p. 273; Phoebe Lapine/Getty, p. 279; Rafael Pranschke/Stockfood, p. 285; Shaun Cato-Symonds/Stockfood, p. 290; Michael Wissing/Stockfood, p. 299; Lauri Patterson/Getty, p. 306; Maja Smend/Stockfood, p. 316; Eising Studio-Food Photo & Video/Stockfood, p. 328; Laura Johansen/Stockfood, p. 336; Larissa Veronesi/Media Bakery, p. 341; Jean-Christophe Riou/Stockfood, p. 344; Tanya Zouev/Stockfood, p. 348; Aniko Lueff Takacs/Stocksy, p. 351; Michael Paul/Stockfood, p. 358; Victoria Firmston/Stockfood, p. 362; Alicia Mañas Aldaya/Stockfood, p. 367; Veronika Studer/Stockfood, p. 370; Leigh Beisch/Stockfood, p. 374 (top left). All other photographs www.shutterstock.com.

ISBN: Print: 978-0-98955-866-2

CONTENTS

INTRODUCTION

Ah, sugar. Sweet, sweet sugar. It makes everything from your morning oatmeal to your after-dinner treats delicious. This may seem innocent enough, but unfortunately, sugar doesn't just sweeten your foods, it also messes with your biology, making you cranky, overweight, and, in a word, sick. In short, consuming refined sugar and excess carbohydrates can lead to mood swings, insomnia, premenstrual syndrome, fatigue, compromised immune function, anemia, depression, anxiety, acne, insulin resistance, type 2 diabetes, heart disease, Alzheimer's disease, and even cancer.

Of course, the "sugar" to be discussed in this book does not just refer to the grainy white substance you stir into your morning coffee, or even the stuff in obvious culprits like ice cream and brownies. Sugar in this book also means the hidden sugar existing in many processed foods, as well as the sugar manufactured by your own body when you eat carbohydrates of any kind.

To make matters worse, numerous studies, including one published in the journal *Current Opinion in Clinical Nutrition and Metabolic Care*, have shown that sugar is in fact more addictive than cocaine. According to studies at Princeton University, rats exposed to sugary foods have demonstrated increased intake, withdrawal, cravings, and relapse, all of which are critical elements of addiction.

This book will explain the science of sugar and how it wreaks havoc with your body's systems, creating a vicious cycle of sugar addiction. The book will demonstrate how detoxing from sugar and carbs will help you lose weight, increase your energy level, lower your risk of disease, and overall, achieve a greater state of good health and contentment. Most important, the book provides a day-by-day guide to kicking your sugar and carbohydrate habit, more than 175 easy and delicious no-sugar recipes, and guidelines to new eating habits that will help you live happily and healthily ever after.

PART I

ARE YOU READY TO QUIT SUGAR?

Quitting sugar won't be easy, not just because most of us enjoy its taste, or because of its addictive nature, but simply because sugar is concealed in so many of the foods we eat that it's difficult to avoid it. But to achieve the benefits of a sugar detox—to overcome your addiction and improve your health—you have to quit it totally and completely.

If you are committed and ready to make a real change in your well-being, then this program is a great place to start.

In Part I, you'll learn all about the science of sugar, and how sugar and refined carbs affect your metabolism. You'll learn the difference between "natural" sugars and refined sugars, and why you shouldn't add either of them to your food. You'll learn about "good carbs" and "bad carbs," and how to fill your plate with the macro- and micronutrients you need to thrive in every way. And you'll learn how to go about breaking your addiction and cleaning out your system.

ONE

SUGAR BASICS

In the days of our ancestors, sugar was only available in naturally occurring forms like fruit and honey, nutrient-dense foods that were limited in availability, both seasonally and geographically. As a result, people consumed far fewer calories from sugar in their diets than we do today. Even just going back a couple hundred years, the difference is astounding. According to the American Heart Association, in 1822, Americans consumed less than 10 grams of sugar per day, or a little more than 2 teaspoons, yet by 2014, sugar consumption had jumped to a shocking 88 grams per day, or 22 teaspoons. That sobering statistic can be explained by the fact that refined sugar is now widely available and that it has made its way into just about everything we eat, from cookies and brownies to salad dressing, yogurt, and tortillas.

The thing is, there is absolutely no benefit to eating sugar. That's right, none at all. You may have heard the age-old diet adage to observe moderation in all things or to avoid eliminating any one food group entirely. But guess what? Sugar isn't a food group, or even a food per se. It is a chemical extracted from plant foods. On its own, it possesses no nutritional value whatsoever. It's not like fat or protein or complex carbohydrates, which all provide nutritional benefits. Sugar is just straight calories with no redeeming qualities, hence the term "empty calories."

In addition to causing long-term ills like weight gain, obesity, type 2 diabetes, and Alzheimer's disease, living in a state of sugar addiction has immediate effects on your day-to-day life, ranging from insomnia, anxiety, and fatigue, to tooth decay, vision problems, frequent urination, and even chronic colds or sinus infections.

And because it is addictive, sugar keeps you trapped in a vicious cycle of craving, consuming, crashing, craving, consuming, crashing . . . as your daily sugar intake goes through the roof.

Quiz: Are You Addicted to Sugar?

Even if you aren't popping candy all day long, and even if you normally skip dessert and say no to treats, you can still be a sugar addict. Take this quiz to find out.

1. Do you crave sugar or sweet foods every day, or even a few times a week?
2. Do you crave starchy foods like bread, pasta, rice, or cereal?
3. Do you like to have something sweet after every meal?
4. Do you start to feel cranky, fatigued, or even weak or shaky if you go more than three hours without eating?
5. Do you drink alcoholic beverages more than once or twice a week?
6. Do you often feel tired in the morning, even when you've gotten a good night's sleep?
7. Do you commonly experience an energy crash in the afternoons?
8. Are you struggling to lose weight on a low-fat diet that's rich in whole grains?
9. Do you drink soda, juice, or other sugary drinks?
10. Are you unable to stop eating after a bite or two of a sugary treat?

If you answered yes to even one of these questions, you are most likely a sugar addict. But don't beat yourself up about it—most of us are addicted to sugar. With so much sugar added to the foods we eat, it's nearly impossible not to succumb to sugar's siren song.

As mentioned earlier, the average American now consumes as much as 22 teaspoons, or 88 grams, of sugar each day. The American Heart Association, meanwhile, recommends a limit of 6 teaspoons, or 24 grams, per day for women and 9 teaspoons, or 36 grams, per day for men. That means that consuming one single-serving container of flavored yogurt, which contains about 10 teaspoons of sugar, would put anyone over their daily limit.

Why Reduced-Fat Foods Might Be Making You Fat

Most of us have been taught that the key to a lean and trim body—and a healthy heart—is a low-fat diet. Food manufacturers have embraced this idea wholeheartedly, producing scads of low-fat or fat-free versions of our favorite foods—from breakfast cereal to cookies. But these foods may be doing us more harm than good.

The first problem with low-fat foods is that they often rely on hydrogenated fats—vegetable oils that have been structurally

The Unfortunate Truth about Diet Soda

Quitting a soda habit is an excellent step toward developing healthier eating habits and losing weight. And reaching for a zero-calorie, sugar-free replacement may seem like a no-brainer. But contrary to what you might expect, researchers at Purdue University have found that consuming diet sodas—even just one a day—can actually contribute to weight *gain* (as well as a higher risk of heart disease, stroke, diabetes, metabolic syndrome, and high blood pressure)!

You'd think that beverages sweetened with calorie-free additives would, at the very least, help to prevent additional weight gain, even if it doesn't assist in weight reduction, but that doesn't appear to be the case. One theory on the connection between diet soda and weight gain is that it's actually a question of mind-set. In other words, by choosing an artificially sweetened, zero-calorie beverage, a person may feel entitled to enjoy other high-calorie foods: "Since I'm having diet soda instead of regular, I can eat a cheeseburger instead of a salad."

Another theory is that artificial sweeteners interfere with the body's learned responses and confuse its ability to manage calorie intake and metabolism. Artificial sweeteners trick your brain into thinking that you've consumed a large dose of calories, or fuel for your body. When that fuel doesn't arrive, your body becomes confused and craves those calories, even if you have just consumed a meal. In other words, drinking a diet soda, even alongside a meal, may increase your appetite and lead you to consume additional calories.

Whatever the reason, skip the soda altogether and choose water or herbal tea instead.

modified to act more like solid saturated fats like lard and butter—to increase the shelf life of packaged foods and improve their flavor and mouthfeel. The hydrogenation process produces dangerous trans fats—which both raise "bad" cholesterol levels and lower "good" cholesterol levels—and many "diet" foods these days are loaded with them.

Secondly, food manufacturers usually load reduced-fat versions of foods with sugar in order to make up for the loss of flavor that results from reducing the fat. Ultimately, many low-fat or fat-free foods are as high, or even higher in calories than their regular counterparts.

To confound the problem, people often feel that choosing a low-fat or fat-free version of a food gives them license to eat twice as much of it. Worse still, foods that are low in fat and high in sugar are more likely to cause spikes in blood sugar and subsequent crashes, leading to increased hunger and binge eating.

Alternatively, eating naturally nutrient-dense foods like nuts and seeds, vegetables, whole grains, and lean meats will fill you up faster, keep you feeling full longer, and ultimately help you far more in controlling your weight and protecting your health than reduced-fat or fat-free substitutes.

How a Sugar Detox Helps

Whether your sugar addiction is raging or mild, a sugar detox can make a huge difference in how you feel and in your overall health. The 28-day programs you'll find in this book will help you reduce or even eliminate completely your sugar (and carbohydrate) cravings. You simply won't feel the urge to reach for the sweet, starchy stuff any longer.

After just four weeks of following a sugar detox diet, you'll likely find that not only will your eating habits have changed, but your palate will react differently to foods, as well. You'll become much more sensitive to naturally occurring sweetness in foods, and foods that once tasted "sweet enough" or perhaps not even sweet at all will begin to taste *very* sweet to you. You may even find that your favorite treats now taste too sweet to you altogether, and you no longer enjoy them.

If you are hoping to shed a few pounds, you'll be happy to hear that even though the sugar detox diet doesn't focus on restricting calories or even tracking them, many people do lose weight by undertaking a sugar detox. This makes sense, since by eliminating sugar and refined carbs, you are automatically eating more nutrient-dense foods that leave you feeling fuller and more satisfied for longer. In the end, you are consuming fewer calories just by virtue of stabilizing your blood sugar.

Most important, undergoing a 28-day sugar detox will give you a nutritional jump start that will make you feel better—you'll have more energy, enhanced concentration, better sleep, clearer skin, among other benefits—and you will also have significantly reduced your risk for certain diseases.

Best of all, you'll be free from the cravings and blood-sugar rollercoaster that have ruled your life for as long as you likely can remember.

TWO

THE MECHANICS
OF SUGAR

To understand sugar addiction, let's first look at what happens inside your body when you consume not just sugar but carbohydrates of any kind. Any food that is not primarily protein or fat is considered a carbohydrate—everything from bread, pasta, and rice to apples, peaches, broccoli, and butternut squash. These foods contain energy in the form of glucose, aka sugar, the portion of these foods your body uses for energy.

The Biochemical Role of Sugar in Your Body

Upon eating any carbohydrate, your body's first task is to break the food down so that it can access the glucose. The glucose is then absorbed into your bloodstream, triggering the release of insulin, a hormone that determines how the body utilizes sugar. In the best-case scenario, glucose is used by your cells for quick energy, and any excess is stored in the liver as glycogen. When the body needs more energy, another hormone called glucagon is released, signaling the liver to convert the glycogen back into glucose.

The worst-case scenario comes about when you consume foods high in refined carbohydrates and added sugars. This causes a "sugar high" wherein extra glucose floods the bloodstream, signaling the pancreas to release more and more insulin. This extra insulin in turn attempts to rectify the situation by telling the liver to produce and store more glycogen, and to stash additional glycogen it can't store in muscle tissue. But those organs have limited storage capacity, and once they've reached their limits, the remaining excess glucose is converted into triglycerides, or fat, which is stored in the body's fat cells.

So if too much sugar is so bad for us, why do we crave sweeter and sweeter foods? That's where the neurotransmitter dopamine comes in. Dopamine is a chemical that controls feelings of reward and pleasure in the brain. There are many things that cause your body to release dopamine, including physical touch, exercise, and sex. Consuming certain substances—including caffeine, narcotics, and, you guessed it, sugar—also releases dopamine.

As the pleasurable feelings created by dopamine begin to wear off, your body is driven to seek more of it. When you set off a dopamine response by occasionally eating naturally occurring sugars in, say, fruit or a bit of honey—foods that deliver micronutrients and fiber along with a hit of glucose—a reasonable amount of those foods would be enough to satisfy the craving, and it's not a problem because those foods are nutrient dense. But according to research by the National Institutes of Health, headed by Dr. Nora Volkow, a leading addiction researcher, when you repeatedly load your system with high-sugar foods, some of your brain's dopamine receptors begin to shut off due to overstimulation. As a result, you need increasingly more and more of those foods to achieve the pleasurable feelings you crave. By regularly indulging in highly processed foods that provide your body with little nutritional value, you are left with nothing more than a persistent, growing desire for more sugar. This is sugar addiction in a nutshell.

Good Carbs, Bad Carbs

Not all carbohydrates are created equal. Simple carbohydrates are composed of just one or two linked sugar molecules. These simple

Nutrient Density

Nutrient density measures the ratio of nutrition to calories in food. Foods that are rich in nutrients and low in calories are said to be nutrient dense. In addition to calories, these foods contain micronutrients—such as B vitamins, phosphorus, magnesium, iron, copper, manganese, zinc, and chromium—that enable your body to utilize the energy of those calories efficiently.

Nutrient-poor foods are foods that offer little in the way of micronutrients but are high in calories. These foods promise your body energy, but can basically be compared to writing a rubber check. Without the micronutrients your body needs to utilize those calories efficiently, they leave you feeling tired and even hungrier than before, contributing to a vicious cycle of blood sugar spikes and crashes.

Nutrition Basics

If you're like most people, you probably don't think all that much about the different components making up the foods you eat. However, a quick lesson can give you a leg up on insuring that you eat the most beneficial foods possible.

CALORIES: Calories are a measurement of how much energy your body derives from a given food. Your body needs calories to function, but there are still good calories and bad calories. The good ones are those coming from nutrient-dense foods that provide a positive ratio of the micronutrients and macronutrients your body needs to maintain optimum health.

MACRONUTRIENTS: There are three macronutrients—protein, fat, and carbohydrates—that contain the calories your body uses for energy. Your body needs each of these, in varying amounts, to function well and maintain optimum health. Proteins are essential for building, maintaining, and repairing body tissue, and are also important for immune function. Fat provides the body with insulation and padding to protect vital organs, and plays a vital role in growth and development. Fat also plays a crucial role in the body's absorption of micronutrients. Carbohydrates are the body's preferred source of energy for the brain, heart, and central nervous system.

MICRONUTRIENTS: These are the vitamins and minerals your body needs to carry out its vital functions, including metabolizing the macronutrients you consume. Micronutrients do not have calories but are an essential part of a healthy diet.

carbs are very easy for the body to break down and digest, and they provide a quick burst of energy and spike in blood sugar, as well as a subsequent sugar crash.

Complex carbohydrates, on the other hand, are composed of several sugar molecules strung together, which means they take longer to break down and digest than simple carbohydrates and therefore provide more sustained energy to the body. Complex carbs are the kind found in vegetables, fruits, nuts, seeds, and grains—foods that are rich in fiber and micronutrients. Because they take longer to break down, they help to maintain a steady blood-sugar level, which is why you experience a sugar crash after eating simple carb foods but not complex carbs.

Sugar is a carbohydrate, but so are kale, broccoli, carrots, and sweet potatoes—all healthy, nutrient-dense foods. So clearly, some carbs are better than others, but how do you know which is which?

You might think that simple carbs are bad and complex carbs are good. Unfortunately, it's not that simple. Even foods made from whole grains, like whole-grain bread, are less nutrient dense than whole foods like brown rice, sweet potatoes, or apples. So when we talk about good carbs and bad carbs, what exactly is the distinction?

One way to approach this question is to think about how much processing a food has undergone, because processing tends to maintain the macronutrients of foods—carbohydrates, fat, and calories—while stripping them of micronutrients. In short, processing and refining turn whole, nutrient-dense foods into calorie-heavy, nutrient-poor foods.

So for the purposes of sugar detox, "good carbs" are those from whole foods. These foods provide not just the calories—or energy—your body needs, but also the micronutrients that allow it to utilize that energy most effectively. These include vegetables, fruits, nuts, seeds, and whole grains (but not whole-grain flours).

TIP **Always Read the Ingredients List!** You may be in the habit of reading the Nutrition Facts portion of food labels to find out the size of a serving, how many calories are in a serving, or how much fat, sodium, or cholesterol the food contains. But if your goal is to eliminate added sugars from your diet, you must read the ingredients list, as well. Doing so reveals that added sugar shows up in the most unlikely foods—in ketchup, mustard, salad dressings, tomato sauces, tortillas, and even dried fruits (like they need *more* sugar?). In addition to the word "sugar," look for the names of other natural, refined, and artificial sweeteners like honey, brown rice syrup, cane syrup, malt syrup, corn syrup/high-fructose corn syrup, dextrose, maltitol, aspartame, saccharin, and sucralose.

A Note about Enriched and Fortified Foods

Many processed foods are labeled as "enriched" or "fortified." These terms refer to the process of adding nutrients to foods to make them more nutritious. Enriching means adding back nutrients that are lost in processing. This is commonly seen in grain-based products like bread or cereal. Fortifying means adding nutrients to a food that didn't contain them to begin with, like when vitamin D is added to milk.

While these terms may sound especially nutritious, keep in mind that foods with synthetic nutrients added to them are not necessarily as nutritious as whole foods containing those nutrients in their natural form. This is because naturally nutrient-dense foods contain multiple nutrients in a careful balance working together to ensure that they are all properly absorbed and utilized in the body.

The Many Names of Sugar

The sugar most commonly found in food is called sucrose, which is actually a combination of two smaller sugars, fructose and glucose. Sucrose is the sugar you find in fruits and vegetables, as well as in table sugar, high-fructose corn syrup, honey, maple syrup, and other caloric sweeteners. Another sugar found in food called lactose—a combination of glucose and galactose—is found in dairy products.

There is also a third type of sugar, but one that, unlike sucrose and lactose, does not occur in food. Maltose is a sugar—made of two glucose molecules strung together—that is manufactured in our bodies when we eat starchy foods like bread, rice, or potatoes.

Natural versus Refined Sugar

You may hear people make a distinction between natural and refined sugars. On a basic level, sugar is sugar. The structure and composition of sugar molecules is the same no matter what type of food they come from, and whether they are found in a whole food or in refined form.

Refined sugar is sugar that has been extracted from plant foods—cane sugar, beet sugar, corn syrup, and so on. Generally speaking, the more a sweetener has been refined or processed, the worse it is for your body. Granulated sugar, brown sugar, and powdered sugar are all refined sugars with zero nutritional value. High-fructose corn syrup and artificial sweeteners are even more processed—made in factories and hardly even resembling food anymore—and are therefore the least desirable sweeteners.

So-called natural sugar is that found in whole foods like fruits, vegetables, and dairy products, as well as honey, molasses, and maple syrup (since these require little to no processing). While the sugar itself is no different—it's still just a simple carbohydrate with no nutritional value—these foods deliver significantly more nutritional value along with their calories. Not only do you get micronutrients that your body needs, but whole foods like fruits and vegetables also contain fiber, which serves to slow digestion of glucose, helping to avert the spike in insulin and subsequent sugar crash you receive from refined sugar.

Sugar by Any Other Name Is Still as Sweet

When you begin to eliminate added sugars from your diet, you soon realize there's more to the story than just nixing foods that list "sugar" on their ingredients list. Following is a list of sweeteners: some are just different names for basic sugar, while others are artificial sweeteners. What they all have in common is that they make food taste sweet and fuel a sugar addiction like nobody's business. All of these sweeteners are off-limits during the sugar detox.

Unrefined Sweeteners
These minimally refined sweeteners are off-limits during the sugar detox, but may be reintroduced in small quantities after the detox.

Dates/date syrup
Fruit juice
Honey
Maple syrup
Molasses

Refined Natural Sweeteners

These sweeteners are derived from natural foods (plants) but are highly refined. These are off-limits during the sugar detox and should be left off the menu afterward as well.

Agave/agave nectar
Brown rice syrup
Brown sugar
Cane juice
Coconut sugar
Corn syrup/high-fructose corn syrup
Dextran
Dextrose
Fructose
Granulated sugar
Malt syrup
Maltitol
Mannitol
Palm sugar
Powdered sugar
Raw sugar
Sorbitol
Sorghum syrup
Stevia
Sucrose
Turbinado sugar
Xylitol

Artificial Sweeteners

Many of these sweeteners have no calories, but nonetheless deliver a sweet flavor that can fuel a sugar addiction and interfere with the body's metabolism. These are off-limits during and after a sugar detox.

Aspartame (Equal, NutraSweet)
Saccharin (Sweet'N Low)
Sucralose (Splenda)

Gluten-Free, Paleo, and Sugar Detox Diets: What's the Difference?

With a new diet-of-the-moment rising to fame seemingly every week, it's hard to keep track of the differences. Paleo, gluten-free, and sugar detox are three popular diets that have one thing in common; they all eschew gluten-containing grains including wheat, barley, and rye. Beyond that, though, the three have very different requirements.

The gluten-free diet is favored by people who believe they have a sensitivity to or inability to tolerate gluten, as well as by sufferers of celiac disease (a rare but serious disease in which the consumption of gluten causes damage to the lining of the small intestine). The gluten-free diet seeks to eliminate all gluten from the diet by not

TIP **Reduce Inflammation for Good Health** Inflammation is one of your body's defense mechanisms against infection and disease. When your body perceives the presence of harmful stimuli—such as damaged cells, irritants, bacteria, viruses, and other pathogens—it produces white blood cells and chemicals to fight those harmful stimuli and prevent infection, heal wounds, and rebuild muscles. The signs of inflammation can include fever, redness, or swelling. When you catch a cold virus, for instance, you may develop a fever (a form of inflammation) while your body attempts to fight it off. But chronic low-grade inflammation can lead to premature aging, eczema, arthritis, asthma, yeast infections, and chronic pain. According to a study in the journal *Preventing Chronic Disease*, inflammation may be at the root of many chronic diseases, from high blood pressure and heart attacks to type 2 diabetes, Alzheimer's, and even cancer.

Both sugar and gluten are inflammatory foods, so it follows that eating these regularly or in excess can put your body in a perpetually inflamed state. By eliminating refined sugars, strictly limiting naturally occurring sugars, and avoiding gluten, you can reduce the inflammation in your body, which can help you not only feel better on a day-to-day basis, but also help you reduce your risk of serious disease in the future.

allowing the gluten-containing grains wheat, barley, and rye. The diet is similar to both the paleo and sugar detox diets only in that it avoids gluten-containing grains. It differs in that it allows non-gluten-containing grains, legumes, dairy products, processed foods, and foods with added sugar.

The Paleo diet seeks to re-create the diet of our ancestors—the diet humans ate when we lived as hunter-gatherers before we developed agricultural practices. As a result, the Paleo diet advocates eliminating all processed foods, all grains, beans, legumes, and dairy products—any food that would not have been available to the cave people. Paleo dieters eat whole fruits, vegetables, raw nuts and seeds, honey, maple syrup, dates/date syrup, and meat. The Paleo diet is favored by athletes who thrive on a high-protein, low-carb diet.

Like the Paleo diet, the sugar detox diet focuses on whole, unprocessed foods—vegetables, fruits, nuts, seeds, and meat. Unlike the Paleo diet, the sugar detox diet allows whole grains (but not grain flours) as well as some legumes and dairy products in limited quantities. Also unlike the Paleo diet, the sugar detox diet focuses on eliminating both added or refined sugars, as well as the sugar manufactured by the body in response to the consumption of starchy foods like potatoes, legumes, gluten-containing grains, and all refined grains. The biggest difference between the Paleo and sugar detox diets is that the Paleo diet permits "natural," unrefined caloric sweeteners like honey, maple syrup, agave nectar, and date syrup, while the sugar detox diet prohibits any added sweeteners.

PART II

YOUR SUGAR DETOX PROGRAM

Now that you understand the nature of sugar, how it functions in your body, and how you become addicted to it, it's time to start breaking your sugar habit. This section details the general guidelines of the 28-day detox program and specifies which foods are off-limits. It presents three different meal plan options (yellow, green, and blue), and shows you how to determine which plan is best for you. It also provides tips for adapting these meal plans to your needs if you have special dietary requirements, such as vegetarian or vegan, for example, or if you have allergies to certain foods.

Next, you'll learn how to prepare for your detox, and get a preview of what to expect in terms of changes to your palate and appetite, as well as challenges you'll likely encounter.

To make your transition as smooth as possible, tips are provided on shopping, cleaning out and stocking your pantry, making substitutions for problematic ingredients, and dining out.

Making a radical change to your dietary habits can be a bumpy ride, so to help you track your progress, stay motivated, and quantify your success, a Success Log in this section allows you to monitor your daily activities: your sleep, moods, appetite, what you're eating, and how much you are exercising.

THREE

CHOOSING THE RIGHT SUGAR DETOX FOR YOU

Whether you've chosen to begin a sugar detox because you want to lose weight, sleep better, have clearer skin, increase your energy, banish cravings, or simply adopt healthier long-term eating habits, the meal plans and recipes that follow will provide the tools you need to achieve your goals.

By following any of the meal plans here, you will gradually adjust both your palate and your eating habits so that not only will you cut high-sugar foods from your diet, but you will also crave them less, and they may quickly come to taste too sweet for your liking.

These plans are designed to make it easy for you to kick the sugar habit by providing you with a list of what to eat for every meal for 28 days, but they are also designed to be flexible. You can modify any of the meal plans to suit your specific needs and tastes. Lists of approved foods give you plenty of substitution options, if some of the items on the plan don't appeal to you.

All three of the meal plans share a few common elements, the most obvious one, of course, being that they do not allow added sugar or artificial sweeteners. This includes "natural" sweeteners like honey, maple syrup, agave nectar, stevia, coconut sugar, molasses, corn syrup, table sugar, and any other sweetener that is added to foods either in processing or at the table.

Gluten is also off the menu in all three of the meal plans, because gluten, like sugar, is inflammatory. Since one of the main goals of sugar detox is to reduce inflammation, eliminating the most obvious causes—sugar and gluten—is essential. Although two of the plans—the yellow and green plans—allow gluten-free whole grains, none allows grain flours of any kind, since refining grains, even whole grains, reduces their nutrient density.

Caffeine is also off-limits on all three plans because it can cause sugar cravings and interfere with healthy sleep habits.

Fruit is limited to small servings of green apples, grapefruit, lemons, limes, and berries. These fruits are allowed, in limited quantities, because they are relatively low in fructose and are loaded with fiber, antioxidants, and other micronutrients. Sweeter fruits are not allowed because fruits that are very high in sugar and taste very sweet

TIP **Fat Adaptation—It's a Good Thing** Contrary to what you may have been led to believe, eating fat doesn't make you fat. In fact, the human body is fully capable of breaking down fat into glucose and using it for energy. This process, however, requires more effort than simply relying on the glucose already circulating in the bloodstream.

Carbohydrate foods provide easy-to-access energy for the body. When you eat a high-carb diet, over time the body comes to rely on this easy energy and prefer it to the energy it has to work harder to access. When this happens, the body ceases to metabolize fat effectively. The body then converts any excess carbs to fat and stores it to be used for energy in the future. Any excess fat you consume is stored as fat, as well, since the body is getting all the energy it needs from easy-to-access carbohydrates. And since you are feeding your body a steady stream of carbohydrates, it never needs to access the fat stores for energy.

When you drastically restrict carbohydrates, however, your body adapts by learning (or, rather, relearning, since this is how our metabolism worked back in the olden days when whole foods were our only option) how to tap into the body's fat stores for energy. When this happens, you are said to be "fat adapted" or "a fat burner" (rather than "a sugar burner"). Fat adaptation is the goal of low-carb diets of all stripes.

can trigger sugar cravings just like candy can. The ultimate goal is to alter your palate so that you no longer crave sweet flavors.

Where the three plans differ is in whether or not they allow dairy products, whole grains (gluten-free), or legumes.

Quiz: Which Sugar Detox Plan Is Right for You?

This book includes three different sugar detox plans—yellow, blue, and red, going from least to most restrictive. This gives you the choice of easing into sugar detox if you are new to it or are going from a high-sugar or high-carb diet. Of course, you can choose whichever plan feels most comfortable to you no matter where you are starting from, but the following quiz is designed to help you determine which plan level will offer you the highest likelihood of success.

1. Is this your first time doing a sugar detox?
    a. Yes.
    b. No, I've done a sugar detox once before.
    c. I have completed two or more sugar detoxes in the past.
2. My sugar and carb cravings are:
    a. Extremely strong. I'm nervous that I won't be able to conquer them.
    b. Very strong, but I'm ready to try to break my addiction.
    c. Fairly mild, but still present.
3. I currently eat:
    a. Bread, pasta, and other foods made from grain flours (including wheat or whole wheat or other grains).
    b. Only gluten-free versions of bread, pasta, or other grain-based foods.
    c. No grains.
4. I currently eat:
    a. Fat-free dairy products such as fat-free yogurt, sour cream, cream cheese, or skim milk.
    b. Low-fat dairy products such as low-fat yogurt, sour cream, cheese, or low-fat milk.
    c. Only full-fat dairy products like whole milk, cheese, butter, and cream or no dairy at all.

....

If most of your answers were "a," the yellow plan is your best choice.
If most of your answers were "b," you are ready for the green plan.
If most of your answers were "c," choose the blue plan.

....

Yellow, Green, or Blue Plan: Which Is Right for You?

Yellow Plan

Choose the yellow plan if you are new to sugar detox and/or making a major dietary or lifestyle change. The yellow plan is less restrictive than the other two, allowing full-fat dairy products, gluten-free whole grains (but not grain flours), and legumes. This approach will make it easier for you to stick to the plan, but will still be enough of a challenge to your usual eating habits to make a difference.

If you are a vegetarian or vegan, this plan will also be the best choice for you. You can replace meat, poultry, and fish with legumes, high-protein grains, and eggs and dairy products (if you are ovo-lacto vegetarian).

On the yellow plan, you'll start the day with a protein-rich breakfast, perhaps two eggs scrambled in butter with spinach and red bell peppers. Lunch might be a big salad with meat or fish, and dinner could be any one of the entrée recipes in this book, perhaps Thai Shrimp Curry (page 221) with brown rice and vegetables. You'll snack on Roasted Red Pepper Garlic Hummus (page 164), and you'll even be able to enjoy a treat like Vanilla Blueberry Coconut Cream Ice Pops (page 340).

Green Plan

The Green plan is an intermediate plan and allows limited amounts of full-fat dairy products but no grains or legumes. Choose the green plan if you've done a sugar detox before or are accustomed to a diet low in simple carbohydrates but you still enjoy a bit of cream in your decaf coffee or an occasional crumble of feta cheese on a salad. This plan will help you break your persistent sugar habit by eliminating grains and legumes along with added sugar while still letting you eat a bit of dairy now and then.

On the green plan, you'll start the day with a protein-rich breakfast, like Quick Butternut Squash and Sausage Hash (page 108) with eggs, lunch on something like a Spicy Asian Shrimp Salad with Jicama (page 112), and for dinner you might enjoy Roasted Chicken Breasts with Mustard and Greens (page 274). A snack of Tamari-Roasted Almonds (page 151) and Apple Coconut Bites (page 347) for a treat will round out your day.

The Blue Plan

The blue plan is the most restrictive, prohibiting all dairy products, grains, and legumes. Choose the blue plan if you've done a couple of sugar detoxes before or are currently following a carb-restricted diet like Paleo or another low-carb or grain-free diet. Because you are already used to restricting carbs, this shouldn't be too much of a stretch for you. This plan calls for the total elimination of not just added sugars, grains, and legumes, but also all dairy products.

A typical blue plan day starts with a protein-rich diet of something like Egg Muffins with Peppers, Onions, and Jalapeño Chiles (page 83). Lunch might be a Curried Chicken Salad Lettuce Wraps with Homemade Mayonnaise (page 126). For dinner, you'll enjoy Pork Chops Stuffed with Spinach and Capers (page 293). Chipotle Guacamole (page 162) with veggie sticks makes a perfect snack, and if you need a treat, you might try a rich Hot Chocolate with Coconut Milk (page 357).

Adapting a Plan for Vegetarian, Vegan, or Allergy-Restricted Diets

Detoxing from sugar if you are a vegetarian or vegan is especially challenging since your food choices are already more limited. Replacing carbohydrate calories with additional protein is an effective approach because protein fills you up, keeps you feeling full, and helps you maintain stable blood-sugar levels. So people without dietary restrictions can just eat more meat, poultry, fish, and eggs. But this obviously doesn't work for vegetarians and vegans. Fear not, however, for the sugar detox diet can be adapted to suit either a vegetarian or vegan diet.

Vegetarians can follow the yellow plan, which includes dairy products, legumes, and grains. Vegetarians should choose high-protein grains like quinoa, or combine legumes and grains in the same meal to create a complete protein. Meat, fish, and poultry can be replaced with eggs, nuts, seeds, or legumes (including tofu).

Vegans can also follow the yellow plan, including legumes and grains, but replacing dairy products with nondairy substitutes like nut milks or nut cheeses. Meat, fish, poultry, and eggs should be replaced with nuts, seeds, and legumes (including tofu). As with the vegetarian adaptation, vegans should choose high-protein grains like quinoa and/or combine grains and legumes for a complete protein.

If you have food allergies, simply eliminate those foods from whichever plan you choose, whether that means no nuts, no soy, no dairy, or what have you. If you suffer from gluten intolerance, you're in luck since all three plans are gluten-free.

Foods to Enjoy

Rest assured, even on the strictest level—the blue plan—the sugar detox diet includes many of the foods you love. Following is a list of foods you can enjoy in unlimited quantities. (Enjoy the selected foods marked with an asterisk in limited quantities because of their relatively high sugar content.)

Vegetables
- Cruciferous vegetables (like broccoli, cauliflower, cabbage, Brussels sprouts)
- Leafy greens (like chard, spinach, lettuce, arugula)
- Other (artichokes, asparagus, beets,* bell peppers, carrots,* celery, chile peppers, cucumbers, eggplant, fennel, garlic, ginger, green beans, jicama, leeks, mushrooms, onions, parsnips,* radishes, rutabagas, shallots, snow peas, sugar snap peas, tomatoes, turnips)
- Summer squashes (zucchini, patty pan, yellow squash)
- Winter squashes (acorn,* butternut,* kabocha,* pumpkin,* spaghetti squash)

Meat, Poultry, Seafood
- Beef
- Chicken
- Cured meats (bacon, Canadian bacon, prosciutto, pancetta)
- Deli meats
- Duck
- Fish (especially salmon, mackerel, and other fatty fishes)
- Lamb
- Pork
- Shellfish
- Turkey

Nuts, Seeds, and Nut or Seed Butters

- Almonds
- Brazil nuts
- Cacao nibs
- Cashews
- Chia seeds
- Flaxseed
- Hazelnuts (filberts)
- Hemp seeds
- Macadamia nuts
- Pecans
- Pine nuts
- Pistachios
- Pumpkin seeds
- Sesame seeds and tahini (sesame paste)
- Sunflower seeds
- Walnuts

Fats

- Animal fats (lard, chicken fat [schmaltz])
- Avocado oil
- Coconut oil or coconut butter
- Flax oil
- Grapeseed oil
- Olive oil
- Sesame oil
- Sunflower seed oil

Fatty Fruit

- Avocados
- Coconut
- Olives

Fruit
- Apples*
- Barely ripe bananas (with some green still in the peel)*
- Berries (blackberries, raspberries, blueberries, and strawberries)*
- Grapefruit*
- Lemons
- Limes

Dairy Substitutes
- Almond milk
- Cashew cheese
- Cashew milk
- Coconut milk
- Hemp milk

Herbs, Spices, Seasonings, and Flavorings

All herbs and spices are allowed; just be sure to read ingredient lists carefully when choosing spice blends since many contain sugar or grain flours.
- Coconut aminos
- Extracts (vanilla, almond)
- Fish sauce
- Mustard (check ingredients to make sure it is sugar-free and gluten-free)
- Vinegars (apple cider, balsamic, wine, sherry)

Foods to Enjoy in Limited Quantities (yellow and green plans only)

Certain foods are allowed in limited quantities on the yellow and green plans, but not on the blue plan.

Legumes
- Beans (pinto, garbanzo, kidney, fava, lima, cannellini, black, Great Northern, lentils, split peas, black-eyed peas)
- Peanuts and peanut butter
- Soy (including tofu, miso, and soy sauce)

Whole, Gluten-Free Grains (not grain flours)

- Amaranth
- Brown rice
- Buckwheat
- Millet
- Oats
- Quinoa
- Sorghum
- Teff

Dairy Products

Only full-fat dairy products are allowed on the sugar detox diet. This is because full-fat dairy products are more nutrient dense than their low-fat or fat-free counterparts. Full-fat milk, cream, butter, and yogurt contain fat-soluble vitamins A, D, E, and K—vitamins that strengthen immunity, neutralize the effects of damaging free radicals, and keep bones healthy. Furthermore, fat helps to slow digestion of the natural sugars in dairy products, which aids in keeping your blood sugar on an even keel.

- Butter
- Cheese
- Full-fat milk and cream
- Ghee (clarified butter)
- Kefir
- Plain unsweetened yogurt
- Sour cream

Foods to Avoid

Following is a list of foods that should be avoided no matter which plan you are on.

Sweeteners

- Artificial sweeteners (saccharin, aspartame, sucralose)
- Caloric sweeteners (table sugar, honey, maple syrup, agave nectar, coconut sugar, molasses, corn syrup)

Grains That Contain Gluten
- Barley
- Rye
- Wheat

Grain Flours
- Amaranth flour
- Arrowroot flour or starch
- Buckwheat flour
- Corn flour, polenta, grits, cornmeal, and corn starch
- Kamut flour
- Millet flour
- Oat flour
- Rice flour (including brown rice flour)
- Teff flour
- Tapioca starch
- Wheat flour

Starchy Vegetables
- Corn
- Beets
- Peas
- Potatoes
- Sweet potatoes
- Tapioca (including tapioca flour or starch)

Sweet Fruits
- Dried fruit (including dates, raisins, and prunes)
- Mango
- Melon (watermelon, honeydew, cantaloupe)
- Pineapple
- Ripe bananas
- Stone fruits (peaches, plums, nectarines, cherries, apricots)

Sugary Beverages
- Alcoholic beverages (wine, beer, liquor)
- Energy drinks
- Fruit juices of any kind (besides lemon or lime)
- Sodas

Caffeinated Beverages
- Black tea
- Coffee
- Green tea

10 Tips for Dealing with Cravings and Sugar Withdrawal

1. *Start the day with a good breakfast.* Your mother was right—breakfast *is* the most important meal of the day. Start out with a nutrient-dense, high-protein breakfast, and you'll set yourself up for success all day long.

2. *Eat protein at every meal.* Protein is the key to balancing blood sugar with insulin and eliminating cravings. Nuts, seeds, eggs, meat, poultry, fish, and legumes are all good sources of protein.

3. *Eat fat at every meal.* Fat—the good kind, of course—makes you feel full, helps balance your blood sugar, and is necessary for absorbing many important micronutrients. Good sources of healthy fats include nuts, seeds, olive oil, coconut (milk, oil, and butter), avocados, and fish.

4. *Snack often.* Eating every few hours helps keep your blood sugar at an even keel, and helps prevent the spikes and crashes that make you crave a quick fix.

5. *Steer clear of temptation.* Just like a recovering alcoholic wouldn't keep booze in the house, a sugar detoxer will find success difficult to achieve when surrounded by off-limit foods. Whenever possible, avoid situations where you know you'll be tempted to cheat. When avoiding the situation isn't possible, plan ahead and show up armed with a strategy for staying on track. For instance, if you're going to a party where you know there will be lots of sweets and other off-limit foods, be sure to eat a good meal before you go, and bring along an approved snack.

6. *Get a good night's sleep.* When your energy flags from lack of sleep, the easiest thing to do is to reach for a high-carb snack for a quick burst of energy. Avoid snacking, and ensure quality sleep by avoiding caffeine, turning off electronic devices an hour before lights-out, and creating a soothing sleep environment.

7. *Exercise.* Just like sugar releases feel-good chemicals in your brain, so does physical exercise. Exercise also helps to reduce stress and anxiety, alleviate depression, and improve sleep—all factors that otherwise cause you to reach for the quick fix of sugar and carbs. Even just 30 minutes a day of exercise—from brisk walking to running, swimming, or dancing—can make a major positive impact on your energy level and your outlook.

8. *Drink lots of water.* Drinking water flushes your system. It also keeps you feeling full and fights dehydration, which can cause your energy to flag. If you get tired of drinking plain water, add a squeeze of lemon or lime, try sparkling water, or switch to herbal tea.

9. *Prepare for emergencies.* Maybe not today, maybe not tomorrow, but some day you'll find yourself stuck in an airport or held up late at the office, and you'll be hungry. When your blood sugar crashes, you'll reach for whatever is most convenient to stop the fall, so make sure you have an emergency snack pack with you at all times. Fill it with good sources of protein and fats, like packets of nuts, seeds, or jerky—beef, turkey, salmon are all great—so you're never at the mercy of a vending machine or fast-food outlet.

10. *Don't cheat! It's easy to rationalize having "just one taste" of a sweet or high-carb treat.* But don't do it. The most important thing in any kind of substance-addiction recovery is to eliminate the addictive substance completely. Just like a recovering alcoholic can't have "just one drink," and a recovering smoker can't take "just one hit," so, too, does a recovering sugar addict need to go cold turkey. Just one brownie or scoop of ice cream will only trigger your intense cravings for more sugar. So do yourself a favor and just say no.

FOUR

GET READY TO DETOX

Detoxing from sugar isn't easy, but the benefits are well worth it. The road to your destination might get a little bumpy, especially in the beginning. Everyone comes to the sugar detox from a different starting point and with different goals. But no matter where you start or what your goals are, you can expect to end the detox with more energy, sharper mental focus, better sleep, and improved mood.

What to Expect

As you move forward on this sugar detox program, you can expect to experience both highs—those moments when you feel so good you want to shout from the mountaintops—and lows—when you'll wonder why you got yourself into this to begin with. Just remember that the end result is all good. If you can get through the tough patches, you'll come out stronger, healthier, fitter, and happier.

One of the many positive effects of the program is the change you will experience in the way you fill your plate. At first, it may feel like a real challenge—you'll be discovering what it means to choose high-quality proteins, healthy fats, and the most nutrient-dense fruits and vegetables. But after 28 days of eating this way, you'll have developed completely new habits. Helping yourself to a healthy mix of proteins, fats, and carbohydrates will become second nature to you.

But perhaps the most interesting—and most life-changing—outcome of detoxing from sugar is the way your palate will change. Your sensitivity to sweet flavors will be intensified. In fact, foods that you never perceived as sweet will begin to taste sweet to you. The best thing about this is that not only will your cravings for sweet flavors diminish, but foods with only small amounts of natural sugar will easily satisfy any urges you do have. That's right, you will no longer even want to devour a bag of cookies or a pile of candy.

Recommended Brands

When shopping for products that are free of sugar and other non-approved ingredients on the sugar detox, you must always read labels, since sugar and refined carbs show up in the most unlikely places. Following is a list of sugar detox–friendly brands that will help steer you in the right direction.

Fats and Cooking Oils
- Artisana
- Kerrygold Butter
- Nutiva
- Pure Indian Foods Ghee
- Tropical Traditions
- Wilderness Family Naturals

Flours
- Bob's Red Mill

Nut Butters
- Justin's
- Marantha
- Sunbutter
- Trader Joe's
- Whole Foods

Canned Coconut Milk
- Chaokoh
- Native Forest
- Thai Kitchen

Jerky
- Paleo Jerky
- Steve's Original
- US Wellness Meats

Spices and Seasonings
- Bragg's Aminos (contains soy)
- Coconut Secret Coconut Aminos
- Penzey's
- Simply Organic

Miscellaneous
- Applegate Farms (meats)
- Cove

- Eden Foods
- Emerald (nuts)
- Grass Fed Traditions (grass-fed meats and soy-free-fed eggs)
- Sea Snacks (seaweed snacks)
- US Wellness Meats
- Wild Planet

Replacements for Common Non-Sugar Detox-Friendly Ingredients

Beginning a sugar detox means revamping not only the way you eat, but the way you cook, as well. You'll need to find substitutions for many common ingredients—like soy sauce (which contains both soy and gluten) and cow's milk. The following chart provides substitution suggestions.

Unfriendly Ingredient	Friendly Substitution
Grain flours	Coconut, almond, or hazelnut flours
Hot or cold breakfast cereals	Nuts and dried coconut with almond or coconut milk
Milk (cow, goat, sheep, soy, or rice)	Almond milk or coconut milk
Soy sauce	Coconut aminos
Store-bought snack, protein, or granola bars	Hard-boiled eggs, jerky, nuts, or nut butters

Finding and Replacing Rare ingredients

A few of the recipes in this book call for ingredients that might be unfamiliar or a bit challenging to find in your area. These ingredients are grain-free, sugar-free substitutes for common pantry staples, and adding them to your pantry can make it much easier for you to stick to the sugar detox diet. These ingredients are usually available at health food or natural foods stores, if not at your regular supermarket, but if you don't have one of these or they aren't easily available, the following chart lists easy substitutions as well as online retailers where you can find them.

Ingredient	Substitute	Retailer
Almond meal/flour	Hazelnut meal/coconut flour	www.nuts.com
Chia seeds	Golden flaxseed	www.nuts.com
Coconut aminos	Bragg's aminos, gluten-free soy sauce	www.vitaminshoppe.com
Coconut flour	Almond flour or other nut flours/meals	www.hodgsonmillstore.com
Coconut oil	Olive oil, grapeseed oil, butter, ghee	www.vitaminshoppe.com
Nutritional yeast	Parmesan cheese	www.vitaminshoppe.com

Prepare Yourself

The likelihood of success at any endeavor can generally be measured by how prepared you are. Take at least a few days before starting your detox to get yourself ready. Below is a checklist for things to do in the days leading up to your detox.

1. Choose a start date at least three days away, and mark it on your calendar.
2. Read about the ways sugar and carbs affect your body chemistry, and set clear goals for completing a sugar detox.
3. Determine which detox plan (yellow, green, or blue) is right for you.

4. Review the lists of foods that are permitted, allowed in limited quantities, and not allowed at all.

5. Make notes about which foods you currently eat that will have to be eliminated, and figure out what you will replace them with.

6. Begin weaning yourself off of caffeine by consuming a bit less each day for several days before your detox start date.

7. Try to limit your intake of sugar and carbs in the days leading up to your start date.

8. Clean out your fridge and pantry. Get rid of any foods that contain off-limit ingredients like sugar, artificial sweeteners, wheat, and grain flours of any kind.

9. Go shopping. Just before your start date, go to the grocery store and load up on approved foods—vegetables, approved fruits, and snack foods, nuts, seeds, nut or seed butters, dairy substitutes, eggs, and meat.

10. Prepare the meals for Day One ahead of time to give you a good start right out of the gate.

Tips for Dining Out

Dining out can present the most difficult challenge to any limited eating plan, but it can be especially tricky during a sugar detox since many of the ingredients you are trying to avoid are hidden. Here are a few ideas to help you get through a restaurant meal without blowing your detox.

1. *Believe it's possible to stick to your plan while dining out.* Don't assume that there won't be anything for you to eat at a restaurant and use that as an excuse to toss your commitment to sugar detox out the window. These days, as more and more restaurants embrace the back-to-basics, farm-to-table approach to food, there are more options than you might expect.

2. *Choose the restaurant wisely.* If possible, choose a restaurant or style of cuisine that is likely to offer the best options, such as grilled fish, chicken, or meat, or salads and lots of vegetables. Sauces in Chinese restaurants are often loaded with sugar, so to be on the safe side, Chinese restaurants are best avoided. Indian and Middle Eastern restaurants, on the other hand, often feature

Success Log

Keeping a success log helps you keep track of your progress as well as pinpoint any problems as they arise. A success log will also give you solid evidence of the positive effects the sugar detox is having on you—in terms of sleep, mood, energy level, and so on—which will help keep you motivated.

DAY # _____

SLEEP

Went to sleep _____

Woke up _____

Total sleep time _____

Quality of sleep: ○ poor ○ fair ○ good ○ excellent

EXERCISE

Activity _____

Duration _____

MOOD (YOUR OVERALL MOOD FOR THE DAY)

○ poor ○ fair ○ good ○ excellent

ENERGY LEVEL (YOUR OVERALL ENERGY LEVEL FOR THE DAY)

○ poor ○ fair ○ good ○ excellent

MEALS

Include quantities such as "1 serving Pork and Cilantro Meatballs," "6 ounces grilled chicken breast," or "½ medium avocado."

Breakfast _____

Lunch _____

Dinner _____

Snacks _____

Water consumed (# of 8-ounce glasses) _____

fresh dishes with lots of vegetables, legumes, and grilled meats. In Japanese restaurants, as well, you can feel confident ordering sashimi or grilled fish dishes (ask the chef to hold the sauce, and bring your own coconut aminos to use in place of soy sauce). Mexican restaurants usually have a salad option—just skip the fried tortilla shell—which one can top with grilled meats, salsas, and guacamole. Thai restaurants offer coconut milk–based curries, which are probably fine, just be sure to ask if there is sugar in the sauce. And their grilled meats are also a good bet.

3. *Plan ahead.* If you can't choose the restaurant, try to check the menu in advance to see if there are any good options. If you can't tell from the menu, call ahead and ask.

4. *Don't be afraid to ask for changes.* If side dishes like pasta, rice, beans, or French fries are included with your dish, ask to substitute steamed vegetables or salad instead. Likewise, if a dish comes topped with cheese, sour cream, or other ingredients not permitted on your plan, ask for them to be left off.

5. *Order wisely.* Choose steamed, poached, grilled, roasted, or broiled dishes instead of those that are fried or sautéed.

6. *Skip the rice and pasta.* If you can't substitute vegetables for refined-carbohydrate foods like pasta and white rice, just ask for these items to be left off your plate.

7. *Avoid foods with sauce.* Sauces are delicious, but they almost always contain off-limits ingredients like sugar or flour. Your safest bet is to avoid foods that come topped with sauce. An exception is fresh salsas, if they are made solely of fresh vegetables and spices. Vinaigrettes, too, can be safe, but do ask about the ingredients since many contain sugar or thickeners.

8. *Be cautious with condiments.* Sugar and flour hide in condiments like relish, ketchup, and barbecue sauce, so be sure to check the labels and find alternatives wherever necessary. Don't be reluctant to bring your own.

9. *Stick to water.* Most restaurant beverages are on the list of foods to avoid, so the best advice is to stick to water. Ask for sparkling water with a wedge of lemon or lime, or herbal tea, if you like.

10. *Skip dessert.* Enough said.

There are three different 28-day sugar detox meal plans—yellow, green, and blue—that each have different requirements. Overall, the plans are quite similar, but the subtle differences mean that your food choices throughout the 28 days will be quite different. The yellow plan is the least restrictive, the green slightly more restrictive, and the blue the most restrictive. Read on for details on how the plans differ.

THE YELLOW PLAN

The yellow meal plan is the least restrictive and allows limited quantities of full-fat dairy products, gluten-free whole grains (but not grain flours), and legumes. Like the other plans, it also includes eggs, meat, poultry, fish, vegetables, and certain fruits.

Whole Grains and Legumes
The yellow plan allows up to ½ cup (cooked) per day of either whole grains or legumes. Grain flours and foods made from grain flours, such as brown rice pasta, are not allowed.

Choose from:

Amaranth
Beans (black, cannellini, fava, garbanzo, lentils, pinto)
Brown or wild rice
Buckwheat
Millet
Quinoa
Sorghum

Dairy Products
Only full-fat dairy products are allowed. There are no set quantity limits on dairy products, but they should be eaten in moderation (1 or 2 servings per day). If possible, choose organic or grass-fed varieties.

Choose from:

Cheese (Cheddar, cottage cheese, cream cheese, feta,
   goat, Gouda, Swiss, etc.)
Milk, cream, or half-and-half (whole fat only)
Sour cream
Yogurt or kefir (plain only)

The Yellow 28-Day Meal Plan

Week One

Day One   BREAKFAST: Apple Cinnamon Smoothie
             LUNCH: Cobb Salad (with 1 ounce blue cheese)
             SNACK: Smoky Chili Cashews
             DINNER: Lamb Chops with Minted Pea Purée
             TREAT: Berries and Cream Parfaits
Day Two   BREAKFAST: Grain-Free Banana Nut Granola Crunch
             LUNCH: Ham and Veggie Roll-Ups
             SNACK: Crispy Lemon-Rosemary Roasted Chickpeas
             DINNER: Indian Butter Scallops
             TREAT: Coconut Snowball Truffles
Day Three BREAKFAST: Red Pepper, Spinach, and Goat Cheese
                Frittata Bites
             LUNCH: Spicy Asian Shrimp Salad with Jicama
             SNACK: Tamari-Roasted Almonds
             DINNER: Spice-Rubbed Grilled Turkey Legs with
                1 ear of fresh corn
             TREAT: Meyer Lemon Pudding
Day Four   BREAKFAST: Cinnamon Apple Muffins
             LUNCH: Lettuce-Wrapped Beef Tacos
             SNACK: Zucchini Pesto Rolls
             DINNER: Stir-Fried Sole with Chiles and Garlic
             TREAT: Vanilla Blueberry Coconut Cream Ice Pops

Day Five	BREAKFAST: Spicy Scrambled Eggs with Sausage
	LUNCH: Spinach Salad with Chicken in a Sun-Dried Tomato and Basil Vinaigrette
	SNACK: Crispy Baked Onion Rings
	DINNER: Stir-Fried Pork with Cabbage and Cashews and ½ cup steamed brown rice
	TREAT: Cinnamon-Spiced Applesauce
Day Six	BREAKFAST: Grain-Free Waffles
	LUNCH: Creamy Chicken Soup with Roasted Garlic
	SNACK: Dijon Deviled Eggs
	DINNER: Thai Beef and Basil Stir-Fry with Carrot Salad and ½ cup steamed brown rice
	TREAT: Berries and Cream Parfaits
Day Seven	BREAKFAST: Eggs Baked in Avocados
	LUNCH: Reuben Roll-Ups
	SNACK: Cauliflower "Popcorn"
	DINNER: Tandoori-Spiced Chicken Breast
	TREAT: Banana Chocolate Almond Ice Cream

Week Two

Day One	BREAKFAST: Red Pepper, Spinach, and Goat Cheese Frittata Bites
	LUNCH: Roasted Brussels Sprout Salad with Crumbled Bacon
	SNACK: Tamari-Roasted Almonds
	DINNER: Lamb Chops with Minted Pea Purée and ½ cup quinoa
	TREAT: Chocolate Mousse
Day Two	BREAKFAST: Grain-Free Hot Breakfast Cereal
	LUNCH: Curried Chicken Salad Lettuce Wraps with Homemade Mayonnaise
	SNACK: Creamy Avocado Spinach Dip with veggie sticks
	DINNER: Seared Sea Scallops with Bacon and Kale over ½ cup farro
	TREAT: Banana Chocolate Shake

Day Three	BREAKFAST: Apple Cinnamon Smoothie
	LUNCH: Fresh Herb Frittata with Peas, Bacon, and Feta Cheese
	SNACK: Barbecue-Flavor Zucchini Chips
	DINNER: Beef Short Ribs Braised in Garlicky Tomato Sauce
	TREAT: Meyer Lemon Pudding
Day Four	BREAKFAST: Vietnamese-Style Omelet
	LUNCH: Grain-Free Falafel Patties with Zucchini
	SNACK: Cinnamon-Spiced Carrot Fries
	DINNER: Pork Chops Stuffed with Spinach and Capers
	TREAT: Crisp Ginger Cookies
Day Five	BREAKFAST: Grain-Free Waffles
	LUNCH: Cobb Salad
	SNACK: Zucchini Pesto Rolls
	DINNER: Brazilian Garlic Lime Shrimp with ½ cup black beans
	TREAT: Coconut Snowball Truffles
Day Six	BREAKFAST: Fluffy Bacon and Chive Egg Puffs
	LUNCH: Avocado and Vegetable Sushi
	SNACK: Dijon Deviled Eggs
	DINNER: Lamb Shanks Braised with Balsamic Vinegar
	TREAT: Cinnamon-Spiced Applesauce
Day Seven	BREAKFAST: Grain-Free Banana Nut Granola Crunch
	LUNCH: Pesto Chicken Salad
	SNACK: Smoky Prosciutto-Wrapped Squash Skewers
	DINNER: Bacon and Mushroom Burgers
	TREAT: Vanilla Blueberry Coconut Cream Ice Pops

Week Three

Day One	BREAKFAST: Eggs Benedict
	LUNCH: Ham and Veggie Roll-Ups
	SNACK: Tamari-Roasted Almonds
	DINNER: Shrimp Baked with Tomatoes and Garlic with ½ cup steamed brown rice or quinoa
	TREAT: Cinnamon-Spiced Applesauce

Day Two BREAKFAST: Smoked Salmon and Egg Sushi

LUNCH: Steak Salad with Chilies, Ginger, and Fresh Basil
with ½ cup beans

SNACK: Crispy Baked Onion Rings

DINNER: Seafood Stew with Garlic Aioli

TREAT: Hot Chocolate with Coconut Milk

Day Three BREAKFAST: Sausage-Crusted Quiche with Swiss Chard

LUNCH: Grain-Free Falafel Patties with Zucchini

SNACK: Crispy Lemon-Rosemary Roasted Chickpeas

DINNER: Tandoori-Spiced Chicken Breast

TREAT: Vanilla Blueberry Coconut Cream Ice Pops

Day Four BREAKFAST: Mexican Quiche Baked in Bell Peppers with
1 ounce grated cheese

LUNCH: Spinach Salad with Chicken in a Sun-Dried
Tomato and Basil Vinaigrette

SNACK: Crispy Pepperoni Pizza Bites

DINNER: Vietnamese Stir-Fried Pork with ½ cup
steamed brown rice

TREAT: Meyer Lemon Pudding

Day Five BREAKFAST: Crispy Cauliflower Pancakes

LUNCH: Lettuce-Wrapped Beef Tacos

SNACK: Smoky Chili Cashews

DINNER: Prosciutto-Wrapped Chicken Stuffed with
Goat Cheese

TREAT: Cocoa Pumpkin Fudge

Day Six BREAKFAST: Banana Berry Smoothie with Chia Seeds

LUNCH: Fresh Herb Frittata with Peas, Bacon, and
Feta Cheese

SNACK: Crispy Lemon-Rosemary Roasted Chickpeas

DINNER: Spicy Chinese Beef in Lettuce Cups

TREAT: Apple Coconut Bites

Day Seven BREAKFAST: Prosciutto and Eggs Baked in
Mushroom Caps

LUNCH: Creamy Chicken Soup with Roasted Garlic

SNACK: Roasted Cauliflower Hummus with veggie sticks

DINNER: Lamb-Stuffed Zucchini with Fresh Mint and
½ cup quinoa

TREAT: Apple Pecan Crisp

Week Four

Day One   BREAKFAST: Sausage-Crusted Quiche with Swiss Chard
LUNCH: Cabbage-Wrapped Thai Spring Rolls
SNACK: Crunchy Multi-Seed Crackers
DINNER: Seared Sea Scallops with Bacon and Kale
    with ½ cup white beans
TREAT: Chocolate Mousse

Day Two   BREAKFAST: Cocoa Banana Smoothie
LUNCH: Fresh Herb Frittata with Peas, Bacon, and
    Feta Cheese
SNACK: Chipotle Guacamole with veggie sticks
DINNER: Creamy Green Chile Chicken with
    ½ cup steamed brown rice
TREAT: Crisp Ginger Cookies

Day Three   BREAKFAST: Spicy Scrambled Eggs with Sausage
LUNCH: Cobb Salad with 1 ounce blue cheese
SNACK: Salmon Salad–Stuffed Cucumber Canapés
DINNER: Turkey Meatloaf with Creole Seasoning
TREAT: Coconut-Filled Chocolates

Day Four   BREAKFAST: Smoked Salmon and Egg Sushi
LUNCH: Spicy Asian Shrimp Salad with Jicama
SNACK: Crispy Baked Onion Rings
DINNER: Lemon-Rosemary Seared Steak with Asparagus
    and Mushrooms with ½ cup quinoa
TREAT: Banana Chocolate Almond Ice Cream

Day Five   BREAKFAST: Quick Butternut Squash and Sausage Hash
LUNCH: Mexican Chicken Salad with Chipotle
    Avocado Dressing
SNACK: Crispy Lemon-Rosemary Roasted Chickpeas
DINNER: Prosciutto-Wrapped Chicken Stuffed with
    Goat Cheese
TREAT: Vanilla Blueberry Coconut Cream Ice Pops

Day Six   BREAKFAST: Eggs Baked in a Bacon Crust
LUNCH: Steak Salad with Chilies, Ginger, and Fresh Basil
SNACK: Olive Tapenade with cucumber rounds
DINNER: Roasted Chicken Breasts with Mustard
and Greens
TREAT: Cinnamon-Spiced Applesauce

Day Seven   BREAKFAST: Apple Cinnamon Smoothie
LUNCH: Seared Tuna Salad
SNACK: Smoky Prosciutto-Wrapped Squash Skewers
DINNER: Lamb Chops with Minted Pea Purée
TREAT: Coconut Snowball Truffles

THE GREEN PLAN

The green plan is an intermediate plan, which permits limited amounts of full-fat dairy products, but does not allow grains or legumes. Like the other two plans, it includes meat, poultry, seafood, eggs, vegetables, and limited quantities of certain fruits.

Dairy Products

Only full-fat dairy products are allowed. There are no set limits on quantities of dairy products, but they should be eaten in moderation (1 or 2 servings per day). If possible, choose organic or grass-fed varieties.

Choose from:

    Cheese (Cheddar, cottage cheese, cream cheese, feta, Gouda, Swiss, etc.)

    Milk, cream, or half-and-half (whole fat only)

    Sour cream

    Yogurt or kefir (plain only)

The Green 28-Day Meal Plan

Week One

Day One	**BREAKFAST:** Cocoa Banana Smoothie
	LUNCH: Cobb Salad with 1 ounce blue cheese
	SNACK: Smoky Chili Cashews
	DINNER: Lamb Chops with Minted Pea Purée
	TREAT: Berries and Cream Parfaits
Day Two	**BREAKFAST:** Grain-Free Banana Nut Granola Crunch
	LUNCH: Ham and Veggie Roll-Ups
	SNACK: Dijon Deviled Eggs
	DINNER: Indian Butter Scallops
	TREAT: Coconut Snowball Truffles

Day Three	**BREAKFAST:** Red Pepper, Spinach, and Goat Cheese Frittata Bites
	LUNCH: Spicy Asian Shrimp Salad with Jicama
	SNACK: Tamari-Roasted Almonds
	DINNER: Spice-Rubbed Grilled Turkey Legs
	TREAT: Meyer Lemon Pudding
Day Four	**BREAKFAST:** Cinnamon Apple Muffins
	LUNCH: Lettuce-Wrapped Beef Tacos
	SNACK: Zucchini Pesto Rolls with 1 ounce goat cheese
	DINNER: Stir-Fried Sole with Chiles and Garlic
	TREAT: Vanilla Blueberry Coconut Cream Ice Pops
Day Five	**BREAKFAST:** Spicy Scrambled Eggs with Sausage with 1 ounce cheese
	LUNCH: Spinach Salad with Chicken in a Sun-Dried Tomato and Basil Vinaigrette
	SNACK: Crispy Baked Onion Rings
	DINNER: Stir-Fried Pork with Cabbage and Cashews
	TREAT: Cinnamon-Spiced Applesauce
Day Six	**BREAKFAST:** Grain-Free Waffles
	LUNCH: Creamy Chicken Soup with Roasted Garlic
	SNACK: Crunchy Multi-Seed Crackers with 1 ounce cheese
	DINNER: Thai Beef and Basil Stir-Fry with Carrot Salad
	TREAT: Berries and Cream Parfaits
Day Seven	**BREAKFAST:** Eggs Baked in Avocados
	LUNCH: Reuben Roll-Ups
	SNACK: Cauliflower "Popcorn"
	DINNER: Tandoori-Spiced Chicken Breast
	TREAT: Banana Chocolate Almond Ice Cream

Week Two

Day One	**BREAKFAST:** Red Pepper, Spinach, and Goat Cheese Frittata Bites
	LUNCH: Roasted Brussels Sprout Salad with Crumbled Bacon
	SNACK: Tamari-Roasted Almonds
	DINNER: Lamb Chops with Minted Pea Purée
	TREAT: Chocolate Mousse

Day Two	BREAKFAST: Grain-Free Hot Breakfast Cereal
	LUNCH: Curried Chicken Salad Lettuce Wraps with Homemade Mayonnaise
	SNACK: Creamy Avocado Spinach Dip with veggie sticks
	DINNER: Seared Sea Scallops with Bacon and Kale
	TREAT: Banana Chocolate Shake
Day Three	BREAKFAST: Banana Berry Smoothie with Chia Seeds
	LUNCH: Fresh Herb Frittata with Peas, Bacon, and Feta Cheese
	SNACK: Barbecue-Flavor Zucchini Chips
	DINNER: Beef Short Ribs Braised in Garlicky Tomato Sauce
	TREAT: Meyer Lemon Pudding
Day Four	BREAKFAST: Vietnamese-Style Omelet
	LUNCH: Grain-Free Falafel Patties with Zucchini with 1 ounce feta cheese
	SNACK: Cinnamon-Spiced Carrot Fries
	DINNER: Pork Chops Stuffed with Spinach and Capers
	TREAT: Crisp Ginger Cookies
Day Five	BREAKFAST: Grain-Free Waffles
	LUNCH: Cobb Salad with 1 ounce blue cheese
	SNACK: Zucchini Pesto Rolls
	DINNER: Brazilian Garlic Lime Shrimp
	TREAT: Coconut Snowball Truffles
Day Six	BREAKFAST: Fluffy Bacon and Chive Egg Puffs
	LUNCH: Avocado and Vegetable Sushi
	SNACK: Dijon Deviled Eggs
	DINNER: Lamb Shanks Braised with Balsamic Vinegar
	TREAT: Cinnamon-Spiced Applesauce
Day Seven	BREAKFAST: Grain-Free Banana Nut Granola Crunch
	LUNCH: Pesto Chicken Salad
	SNACK: Smoky Prosciutto-Wrapped Squash Skewers
	DINNER: Bacon and Mushroom Burgers with 1 ounce cheese
	TREAT: Vanilla Blueberry Coconut Cream Ice Pops

Week Three

Day One   BREAKFAST: Eggs Benedict
LUNCH: Ham and Veggie Roll-Ups
SNACK: Tamari-Roasted Almonds
DINNER: Shrimp Baked with Tomatoes and Garlic
TREAT: Cinnamon-Spiced Applesauce

Day Two   BREAKFAST: Smoked Salmon and Egg Sushi
LUNCH: Steak Salad with Chilies, Ginger, and Fresh Basil
SNACK: Crispy Baked Onion Rings
DINNER: Seafood Stew with Garlic Aioli
TREAT: Hot Chocolate with Coconut Milk

Day Three   BREAKFAST: Sausage-Crusted Quiche with Swiss Chard
with 1 ounce Gruyère cheese
LUNCH: Grain-Free Falafel Patties with Zucchini
SNACK: Smoky Prosciutto-Wrapped Squash Skewers
DINNER: Tandoori-Spiced Chicken Breast
TREAT: Vanilla Blueberry Coconut Cream Ice Pops

Day Four   BREAKFAST: Mexican Quiche Baked in Bell Peppers
with 1 ounce grated cheese
LUNCH: Spinach Salad with Chicken in a Sun-Dried
Tomato and Basil Vinaigrette
SNACK: Crispy Pepperoni Pizza Bites
DINNER: Vietnamese Stir-Fried Pork
TREAT: Meyer Lemon Pudding

Day Five   BREAKFAST: Crispy Cauliflower Pancakes
LUNCH: Lettuce-Wrapped Beef Tacos
SNACK: Smoky Chili Cashews
DINNER: Prosciutto-Wrapped Chicken Stuffed with
Goat Cheese
TREAT: Cocoa Pumpkin Fudge

Day Six   BREAKFAST: Banana Berry Smoothie with Chia Seeds
LUNCH: Fresh Herb Frittata with Peas, Bacon, and
Feta Cheese
SNACK: Chipotle Guacamole with veggie sticks
DINNER: Spicy Chinese Beef in Lettuce Cups
TREAT: Apple Coconut Bites

Day Seven BREAKFAST: Prosciutto and Eggs Baked in
Mushroom Caps
LUNCH: Creamy Chicken Soup with Roasted Garlic
SNACK: Crunchy Multi-Seed Crackers with
1 ounce cheese
DINNER: Lamb-Stuffed Zucchini with Fresh Mint
TREAT: Apple Pecan Crisp

Week Four

Day One BREAKFAST: Sausage-Crusted Quiche with Swiss Chard
LUNCH: Cabbage-Wrapped Thai Spring Rolls
SNACK: Roasted Cauliflower Hummus with veggie sticks
DINNER: Seared Sea Scallops with Bacon and Kale
TREAT: Chocolate Mousse

Day Two BREAKFAST: Cocoa Banana Smoothie
LUNCH: Fresh Herb Frittata with Peas, Bacon, and
Feta Cheese
SNACK: Barbecue-Flavor Zucchini Chips
DINNER: Creamy Green Chile Chicken
TREAT: Crisp Ginger Cookies

Day Three BREAKFAST: Spicy Scrambled Eggs with Sausage
LUNCH: Cobb Salad with 1 ounce blue cheese
SNACK: Salmon Salad–Stuffed Cucumber Canapés
DINNER: Turkey Meatloaf with Creole Seasoning
TREAT: Coconut-Filled Chocolates

Day Four BREAKFAST: Smoked Salmon and Egg Sushi
LUNCH: Spicy Asian Shrimp Salad with Jicama
SNACK: Crispy Baked Onion Rings
DINNER: Lemon-Rosemary Seared Steak with
Asparagus and Mushrooms
TREAT: Banana Chocolate Almond Ice Cream

Day Five BREAKFAST: Quick Butternut Squash and Sausage Hash
LUNCH: Mexican Chicken Salad with Chipotle
Avocado Dressing
SNACK: Cinnamon-Spiced Carrot Fries
DINNER: Prosciutto-Wrapped Chicken Stuffed with
Goat Cheese
TREAT: Vanilla Blueberry Coconut Cream Ice Pops

Day Six	BREAKFAST: Eggs Baked in a Bacon Crust
	LUNCH: Steak Salad with Chilies, Ginger, and Fresh Basil
	SNACK: Olive Tapenade with cucumber rounds and 1 ounce feta cheese
	DINNER: Roasted Chicken Breasts with Mustard and Greens
	TREAT: Cinnamon-Spiced Applesauce
Day Seven	BREAKFAST: Eggs Benedict
	LUNCH: Seared Tuna Salad
	SNACK: Smoky Prosciutto-Wrapped Squash Skewers
	DINNER: Lamb Chops with Minted Pea Purée
	TREAT: Coconut Snowball Truffles

THE BLUE PLAN

The blue plan is the most restrictive of the three plans, prohibiting all dairy products, grains, and legumes. Like the other two plans, it includes eggs, meat, poultry, seafood, vegetables, and limited quantities of certain fruits.

The Blue 28-Day Meal Plan

Week One

Day One
BREAKFAST: Cocoa Banana Smoothie
LUNCH: Cobb Salad
SNACK: Smoky Chili Cashews
DINNER: Lamb Chops with Minted Pea Purée
TREAT: Berries and Cream Parfaits

Day Two
BREAKFAST: Grain-Free Banana Nut Granola Crunch
LUNCH: Ham and Veggie Roll-Ups
SNACK: Dijon Deviled Eggs
DINNER: Thai Shrimp Curry
TREAT: Coconut Snowball Truffles

Day Three
BREAKFAST: Sausage-Crusted Quiche with Swiss Chard
LUNCH: Spicy Asian Shrimp Salad with Jicama
SNACK: Tamari-Roasted Almonds
DINNER: Spice-Rubbed Grilled Turkey Legs
TREAT: Meyer Lemon Pudding

Day Four
BREAKFAST: Cinnamon Apple Muffins
LUNCH: Lettuce-Wrapped Beef Tacos
SNACK: Zucchini Pesto Rolls
DINNER: Stir-Fried Sole with Chiles and Garlic
TREAT: Vanilla Blueberry Coconut Cream Ice Pops

Day Five
BREAKFAST: Spicy Scrambled Eggs with Sausage
LUNCH: Spinach Salad with Chicken in a Sun-Dried Tomato and Basil Vinaigrette
SNACK: Crispy Baked Onion Rings
DINNER: Stir-Fried Pork with Cabbage and Cashews
TREAT: Apple Coconut Bites

Day Six	BREAKFAST: Crispy Cauliflower Pancakes
	LUNCH: Creamy Chicken Soup with Roasted Garlic
	SNACK: Crunchy Multi-Seed Crackers
	DINNER: Thai Beef and Basil Stir-Fry with Carrot Salad
	TREAT: Berries and Cream Parfaits
Day Seven	BREAKFAST: Eggs Baked in Avocados
	LUNCH: Seared Tuna Salad
	SNACK: Cauliflower "Popcorn"
	DINNER: Tandoori-Spiced Chicken Breast
	TREAT: Banana Chocolate Almond Ice Cream

Week Two

Day One	BREAKFAST: Cinnamon Apple Muffins
	LUNCH: Roasted Brussels Sprout Salad with Crumbled Bacon
	SNACK: Tamari-Roasted Almonds
	DINNER: Lamb Chops with Minted Pea Purée
	TREAT: Chocolate Mousse
Day Two	BREAKFAST: Grain-Free Hot Breakfast Cereal
	LUNCH: Curried Chicken Salad Lettuce Wraps with Homemade Mayonnaise
	SNACK: Creamy Avocado-Spinach Dip with veggie sticks
	DINNER: Seared Sea Scallops with Bacon and Kale
	TREAT: Banana Chocolate Shake
Day Three	BREAKFAST: Banana Berry Smoothie with Chia Seeds
	LUNCH: Lemon-Lime Shrimp Ceviche with Avocado
	SNACK: Barbecue-Flavor Zucchini Chips
	DINNER: Beef Short Ribs Braised in Garlicky Tomato Sauce
	TREAT: Meyer Lemon Pudding
Day Four	BREAKFAST: Vietnamese-Style Omelet
	LUNCH: Grain-Free Falafel Patties with Zucchini
	SNACK: Cinnamon-Spiced Carrot Fries
	DINNER: Pork Chops Stuffed with Spinach and Capers
	TREAT: Crisp Ginger Cookies

Day Five	BREAKFAST: Quick Butternut Squash and Sausage Hash
	LUNCH: Cobb Salad
	SNACK: Zucchini Pesto Rolls
	DINNER: Brazilian Garlic-Lime Shrimp
	TREAT: Coconut Snowball Truffles
Day Six	BREAKFAST: Fluffy Bacon and Chive Egg Puffs
	LUNCH: Avocado and Vegetable Sushi
	SNACK: Dijon Deviled Eggs
	DINNER: Lamb Shanks Braised with Balsamic Vinegar
	TREAT: Crisp Ginger Cookies
Day Seven	BREAKFAST: Grain-Free Banana Nut Granola Crunch
	LUNCH: Pesto Chicken Salad
	SNACK: Smoky Prosciutto-Wrapped Squash Skewers
	DINNER: Bacon and Mushroom Burgers
	TREAT: Vanilla Blueberry Coconut Cream Ice Pops

Week Three

Day One	BREAKFAST: Banana Berry Smoothie with Chia Seeds
	LUNCH: Ham and Veggie Roll-Ups
	SNACK: Tamari-Roasted Almonds
	DINNER: Shrimp Baked with Tomatoes and Garlic
	TREAT: Chocolate Mousse
Day Two	BREAKFAST: Smoked Salmon and Egg Sushi
	LUNCH: Steak Salad with Chilies, Ginger, and Fresh Basil
	SNACK: Crispy Baked Onion Rings
	DINNER: Seafood Stew with Garlic Aioli
	TREAT: Hot Chocolate with Coconut Milk
Day Three	BREAKFAST: Sausage-Crusted Quiche with Swiss Chard
	LUNCH: Grain-Free Falafel Patties with Zucchini
	SNACK: Smoky Prosciutto-Wrapped Squash Skewers
	DINNER: Tandoori-Spiced Chicken Breast
	TREAT: Vanilla Blueberry Coconut Cream Ice Pops
Day Four	BREAKFAST: Mexican Quiche Baked in Bell Peppers
	LUNCH: Spinach Salad with Chicken in a Sun-Dried Tomato and Basil Vinaigrette
	SNACK: Crispy Pepperoni Pizza Bites
	DINNER: Vietnamese Stir-Fried Pork
	TREAT: Meyer Lemon Pudding

Day Five	BREAKFAST: Crispy Cauliflower Pancakes
	LUNCH: Lettuce-Wrapped Beef Tacos
	SNACK: Smoky Chili Cashews
	DINNER: Seafood Stew with Garlic Aioli
	TREAT: Cocoa Pumpkin Fudge
Day Six	BREAKFAST: Banana Berry Smoothie with Chia Seeds
	LUNCH: Spinach Salad with Chicken in a Sun-Dried Tomato and Basil Vinaigrette
	SNACK: Chipotle Guacamole with veggie sticks
	DINNER: Spicy Chinese Beef in Lettuce Cups
	TREAT: Apple Coconut Bites
Day Seven	BREAKFAST: Prosciutto and Eggs Baked in Mushroom Caps
	LUNCH: Creamy Chicken Soup with Roasted Garlic
	SNACK: Crunchy Multi-Seed Crackers
	DINNER: Lamb-Stuffed Zucchini with Fresh Mint
	TREAT: Meyer Lemon Pudding

Week Four

Day One	BREAKFAST: Sausage-Crusted Quiche with Swiss Chard
	LUNCH: Cabbage-Wrapped Thai Spring Rolls
	SNACK: Roasted Cauliflower Hummus with veggie sticks
	DINNER: Seared Sea Scallops with Bacon and Kale
	TREAT: Chocolate Mousse
Day Two	BREAKFAST: Cocoa Banana Smoothie
	LUNCH: Fresh Herb Frittata with Peas, Bacon, and Feta Cheese
	SNACK: Barbecue-Flavor Zucchini Chips
	DINNER: Creamy Green Chile Chicken
	TREAT: Crisp Ginger Cookies
Day Three	BREAKFAST: Spicy Scrambled Eggs with Sausage
	LUNCH: Cobb Salad
	SNACK: Salmon Salad–Stuffed Cucumber Canapés
	DINNER: Turkey Meatloaf with Creole Seasoning
	TREAT: Coconut-Filled Chocolates

Day Four	**BREAKFAST:** Smoked Salmon and Egg Sushi
	LUNCH: Spicy Asian Shrimp Salad with Jicama
	SNACK: Crispy Baked Onion Rings
	DINNER: Lemon-Rosemary Seared Steak with Asparagus and Mushrooms
	TREAT: Banana Chocolate Almond Ice Cream
Day Five	**BREAKFAST:** Quick Butternut Squash and Sausage Hash
	LUNCH: Mexican Chicken Salad with Chipotle Avocado Dressing
	SNACK: Cinnamon-Spiced Carrot Fries
	DINNER: Pork and Cilantro Meatballs
	TREAT: Vanilla Blueberry Coconut Cream Ice Pops
Day Six	**BREAKFAST:** Eggs Baked in a Bacon Crust
	LUNCH: Steak Salad with Chilies, Ginger, and Fresh Basil
	SNACK: Olive Tapenade with cucumber rounds
	DINNER: Roasted Chicken Breasts with Mustard and Greens
	TREAT: Banana Chocolate Shake
Day Seven	**BREAKFAST:** Grain-Free Banana Nut Granola Crunch
	LUNCH: Seared Tuna Salad
	SNACK: Smoky Prosciutto-Wrapped Squash Skewers
	DINNER: Lamb Chops with Minted Pea Purée
	TREAT: Coconut Snowball Truffles

When you've finished the 28-day sugar detox meal plan, you will likely feel incredibly proud of yourself, as you should! Take some time to bask in the glow of your accomplishment. Changing your eating habits so drastically—not to mention going cold turkey on your drug of choice—is no small feat. You should be very proud of making it through.

You may also feel a strong sense of relief. Now that you have made it through, you can let your guard down and stop being so vigilant about every morsel you put into your mouth. You may be raring to go out and indulge in all the foods you've been missing. But before you do that, take some time to reflect on how much better you feel. Do you have more energy? Are you sleeping better? Have you lost weight, lowered your blood pressure, lowered your blood glucose level, achieved clearer skin, or accomplished any of the other goals you may have started out with? Doesn't it feel empowering not to have your life controlled by sugar and carb cravings? If you are having trouble judging how much better you feel, look through your success log and see how your responses have changed from the first days to the the recent ones. Now ask yourself: Do you really want to throw all of that away just to gorge on an ice cream sundae or a pile of cookies?

Keep the Momentum Going

Now that you have completed the detox, you've developed some entirely new—and healthier—eating habits. While you no longer need to follow a meal-by-meal plan, don't let those good habits fall by the wayside. Continue to focus your meals on high-quality proteins, fats, and vegetables.

Make a note of the recipes from the meal plan that you enjoyed and come back to them again and again. Flip through the recipe section again now and make a note of any recipes you haven't yet tried that look appealing. You can also search the Internet and other sugar-free or low-carb cookbooks for recipes and ideas to keep you on the right track.

Reintroducing Foods

If you were eating bread, pasta, cereal, and other high-carb foods before the detox, then this has been a huge change, not just in your habits, but physically, as well. Your body has actually gone through a withdrawal period, and you may react badly to these foods if you go back to eating them again. It's possible that eating these foods now will have such an unpleasant physical effect that you won't want to revisit them after all.

If you do choose to try reintroducing some of these foods, do so carefully and systematically. Select one food to reintroduce at a time. Eat that food with all three of your meals on the day of reintroduction, and then abstain from that food for an additional two days. Over the three days following the day that you ate the food in question, pay attention to any physical reactions, including effects on your digestion, appetite, and general physical well-being (does it cause headaches, gas, bloating, sleep disturbances, pimples, etc.), as well as your energy level and mood. This information will be your guide to whether you want to reincorporate that food into your day-to-day diet.

If you have a bad reaction to a food, your body is telling you that this particular food isn't good for you. The best approach in that scenario is to eliminate that food from your diet as much as possible. If this is a food you'll really miss, you might try the experiment again at a later time, but that food probably was causing you problems all along and you weren't aware of the cause-and-effect sequence, so just be glad you now know its effect and can avoid it.

Once you have reintroduced one food and determined your reaction, if any, you can try reintroducing another food. This process can take time, but it is the only way to isolate a food and test whether it is affecting you in a negative way. The process is also the way to establish whether you are allergic to any of these foods.

Ultimately, you may decide to begin including some of these foods in your diet again—whether it's because they have little or no effect on how you feel, or you simply enjoy them too much to give them up completely, or because keeping them off-limits is just too inconvenient. Even if you do go back to some of these foods, there's no reason for you to go back to overdoing them, or being a slave to your addiction. You might decide that brownies are just not worth giving up entirely, for instance, but now instead of eating a sweet treat several times a day, you'll have a brownie once a week.

A few reminders: If you reincorporate fruits into your diet, always remember to eat them in combination with protein and fat to keep your blood sugar at an even keel. If you reintroduce starchy foods, eat them in limited quantities, as an accent to a meal rather than the foundation.

The bottom line is that while sugar and starch can be successfully reintroduced into your diet, don't go off the deep end and consumer large portions of pasta and sweets just because the detox is over. You won't want to waste all your hard work completing the successful sugar detox.

PART III

THE RECIPES

If you're used to relying on take-out and frozen meals, the idea of cooking for yourself for 28 days may seem daunting. Even if you're a good cook, you may be slightly intimidated by the new techniques you'll need to learn without many of your old standby ingredients. But don't worry. The recipes in the book are easy to prepare, and the ingredients lists are intentionally brief to limit the amount of specialty-food shopping you need to do. Better still, prep times are generally less than 30 minutes, and many dishes can be made ahead of time, or the leftovers can be kept for another meal. So even if you have little time to devote to cooking, the dishes are totally doable.

The recipes presented here are all made without any added sweeteners or gluten or any other ingredients prohibited on the sugar detox program. Do note, however, that some recipes suitable for the yellow and green level meal plans are not permissible for the blue level, so be sure to check. The meal plan levels that apply to each recipe are clearly marked, along with the nutritional information for each dish.

SEVEN

BREAKFAST

Apple Cinnamon Smoothie

SERVES I   PREP TIME: 5 MINUTES   COOK TIME: NONE

A smoothie makes a great on-the-go breakfast, since it takes only a few minutes to whip up, and you can easily transport it in a travel cup on your commute. Made with tart green apples and cinnamon, this protein-packed smoothie tastes just like apple pie in a glass. Almond butter thickens it and provides a healthy dose of protein.

1 cup ice cubes

½ cup water

½ cup full-fat coconut milk

¼ cup old-fashioned rolled oats, soaked overnight in water and drained

2 tablespoons almond butter

½ green apple, cored and diced

½ teaspoon cinnamon

½ teaspoon nutmeg

Place all of the ingredients in a blender, and blend on medium speed for a minute or two, and then on high speed for an additional minute, until smooth. Serve immediately.

Cocoa Banana Smoothie

SERVES I   PREP TIME: 5 MINUTES   COOK TIME: NONE

Banana gives this smoothie just a hint of sweetness without any added sweeteners. Thickened with chia seeds, this rich and chocolatey, high-protein, high-fiber smoothie is an extremely satisfying breakfast.

1 tablespoon chia seeds

¼ cup water

1 frozen barely ripe banana, cut into chunks

2 tablespoons almond butter

2 tablespoons unsweetened cocoa powder

1 cup almond milk

1. Soak the chia seeds in the water for 10 minutes.

2. Place the chia seeds and any remaining liquid and all the remaining ingredients in a blender. Blend first on medium speed for 1 to 2 minutes, and then on high speed for 1 additional minute, until smooth. Serve immediately.

TIP   For an extra-thick consistency, slice and freeze the banana overnight before making this smoothie.

Perfect Grain-Free Banana Pancakes

SERVES 4 PREP TIME: 5 MINUTES   COOK TIME: 15 MINUTES

● ● ●   *Made without grain, dairy, or refined sugars, these pancakes are perfect for a lazy Sunday morning breakfast with the family. Bananas add flavor and moisture, making added sweeteners like honey or maple syrup unnecessary. Top with chopped nuts, fresh berries, or a dollop of plain yogurt (if you are on the yellow or green plan).*

2 cups almond flour
2 barely ripe bananas, mashed
4 eggs
½ cup water
1 tablespoon coconut oil, plus 1 teaspoon
Pinch of salt

1. In a large bowl, add the almond flour, bananas, eggs, water, 1 teaspoon of the coconut oil, and salt, and stir until well combined and smooth.

2. Heat some of the remaining tablespoon of coconut oil in a large skillet over medium-high heat.

3. Ladle the batter into the pan, about ¼ cup at a time. Cook until bubbles start to appear on the top, for about 2 minutes, then flip the pancakes over and cook until golden on the other side, for about 2 minutes. Repeat until all of the batter has been cooked, adding more of the remaining coconut oil between batches as needed.

4. Serve immediately.

Grain-Free Banana Nut Granola Crunch

SERVES 10   PREP TIME: 5 MINUTES   COOK TIME: 25 MINUTES

● ● ● *Far more satisfying than a bowl of breakfast cereal, this crunchy grain-free granola makes a delicious quick breakfast when served in a bowl of coconut or almond milk. It's also tasty on its own as a snack or sprinkled over plain yogurt (if you're on the yellow or green plan). Use any mixture of nuts you like—choose from almonds, walnuts, pecans, macadamias, or hazelnuts.*

Cooking spray for the pan
½ cup almond meal
1 cup unsweetened shredded coconut
½ cup sunflower seeds
2½ cups mixed nuts
2 barely ripe bananas, cut into chunks
½ cup coconut oil
1 egg
2 teaspoons ground cinnamon
2 teaspoons vanilla extract
¼ teaspoon salt

1. Preheat the oven to 350° F. Coat a large baking sheet with cooking spray.

2. In a large bowl, add the almond meal, coconut, and sunflower seeds, and mix to combine well.

3. In a food processor or blender, process the nuts until they are coarsely chopped. Add to the seed mixture.

4. In the food processor, add the bananas, coconut oil, egg, cinnamon, vanilla, and salt, and process until puréed. Transfer the mixture to the bowl with the nuts and seeds, and stir to mix well.

5. Spread the mixture in an even layer on the prepared baking sheet, and bake for about 30 minutes, tossing every 10 minutes, until lightly browned and crisp.

6. Let cool before serving. Serve at room temperature. Store leftovers in the refrigerator in an airtight container for up to 1 week.

Grain-Free Waffles

SERVES 4   PREP TIME: 5 MINUTES   COOK TIME: 5 MINUTES

With just four ingredients, these crispy waffles are a quick and easy breakfast that's full of protein. Top them with berries or sliced barely ripe bananas, if you like. Best of all, they freeze well, so you can make a big batch and have them on hand for a grab-and-go morning meal any time.

Coconut oil for the waffle iron
6 eggs
⅛ teaspoon cream of tartar
6 ounces cream cheese, at room temperature

1. Preheat the waffle iron and brush with coconut oil.

2. Separate the eggs, placing the whites and yolks in separate medium bowls.

3. Beat the egg whites and cream of tartar together for 3 to 5 minutes, until stiff peaks form.

4. Whisk together the egg yolks and cream cheese. Add the egg white mixture to the egg yolk mixture, and gently fold the two mixtures together until just combined.

5. Pour the batter ¼ cup at a time into the waffle maker, and cook according to the manufacturer's instructions.

6. Serve hot.

TIP   These waffles can be frozen and reheated in the toaster for a quick breakfast. To store, cool to room temperature, then freeze on a baking sheet. When frozen, transfer to resealable freezer-safe plastic bags, and store in the freezer for up to 3 months. They toast quickly, so set the toaster on a light setting and watch carefully.

Banana Berry Smoothie with Chia Seeds

SERVES I   PREP TIME: 5 MINUTES   COOK TIME: NONE

● ● ●   *Chia seeds add a subtle nutty flavor along with a big boost of nutrition. They'll also give the smoothie a nice, thick texture. Using frozen strawberries eliminates the need to add ice cubes. Including both chia and flaxseed, as well as almond butter, gives this smoothie all the protein you need to get your day started.*

1 tablespoon chia seeds
½ cup cold water
1 barely ripe banana, cut into chunks
¾ cup frozen strawberries
1 tablespoon flaxseed
1 tablespoon almond butter

1. Soak the chia seeds in the water for 10 minutes.

2. Place the chia seeds with any remaining liquid and all the remaining ingredients in the blender, and blend first on medium speed for 1 to 2 minutes, then on high speed for 1 additional minute, until smooth. Serve immediately.

TIP   Chia seeds are a superfood. They're loaded with omega-3 fatty acids, with almost 5 grams in a serving. Plus they absorb 10 times their weight in water, forming a bulky gel that can help you feel full and slow down your body's conversion of carbohydrates into simple sugars, which helps to stabilize blood sugar.

Cinnamon Apple Muffins

MAKES 12 MUFFINS   PREP TIME: 5 MINUTES   COOK TIME: 20 MINUTES

Some days, all you want to do on your way out the door is grab a muffin. These slightly spicy, not-very-sweet muffins fit the bill nicely and are the perfect accompaniment to a cup of herbal tea.

¼ cup coconut oil, melted, plus 1 tablespoon,
 plus more for the pan, if needed
2 green apples, cored, peeled, and diced
½ cup coconut flour
⅔ cup almond flour
1 teaspoon baking soda
2 teaspoons ground cinnamon
¼ teaspoon salt
6 eggs
1 teaspoon vanilla extract
⅔ cup coconut milk
1 teaspoon apple cider vinegar

1. Preheat the oven to 350°F. Brush a 12-cup muffin tin with coconut oil or line with paper liners.

2. Heat 1 tablespoon of the coconut oil in a medium skillet over medium-high heat. Add the apple and cook, stirring occasionally, until softened, for about 6 minutes. Set aside to cool.

3. In a large bowl, whisk together the coconut flour, almond flour, baking soda, cinnamon, and salt. ▶

4. In a medium bowl, whisk together the eggs, vanilla, coconut milk, vinegar and the remaining ¼ cup of coconut oil. Add the egg mixture to the flour mixture and stir, until the batter is smooth. Stir in the cooled apples.

5. Spoon the batter evenly into the 12 muffin cups. Bake in the preheated oven for 12 to 14 minutes, until lightly browned and springy to the touch. Transfer to a wire rack to cool, and serve warm or at room temperature.

Egg Muffins with Peppers, Onions, and Jalapeño Chiles

SERVES 12   PREP TIME: 5 MINUTES   COOK TIME: 25 MINUTES

These tasty egg muffins are full of protein and healthy veggies. They are simple to make and keep well in the fridge or freezer. Just pop them in the microwave for a couple of minutes to reheat. If you are on the yellow or green plan, you can even add ½ cup of shredded Cheddar cheese to the beaten eggs, if you like.

1 tablespoon coconut oil, plus more for the muffin tin

1 medium onion, diced

2 cloves garlic, minced

1 green bell pepper, diced

1 red bell pepper, diced

1 jalapeño pepper, seeded and finely diced

12 eggs

1 teaspoon salt

½ teaspoon freshly ground black pepper

1. Preheat the oven to 350° F. Brush a 12-cup muffin tin with coconut oil.

2. Heat the tablespoon of coconut oil in a large skillet over medium-high heat. Add the onion and garlic and cook, stirring occasionally, for abut 4 minutes, until they begin to soften. Add the green bell pepper, red bell pepper, and jalapeño and cook for about 3 minutes, until softened. Remove from the heat and let cool for 2 minutes.

3. Whisk the eggs in a large bowl with the salt and pepper. Add the veggie mixture and stir to mix well.

4. Ladle the egg mixture into the prepared muffin tin, dividing equally. Bake for 10 to 15 minutes, until puffed and golden. Serve hot.

Grain-Free
Hot Breakfast Cereal

SERVES 2   PREP TIME: 2 MINUTES   COOK TIME: I0 MINUTES

● ● ● *When you are lamenting the void in your life created by giving up oatmeal, this hearty, stick-to-your-ribs hot cereal is just the thing. Top it with toasted nuts, fresh berries, or almond or coconut milk, if you like.*

1 barely ripe banana, mashed

3 eggs

¼ cup almond or coconut milk

1 teaspoon vanilla extract

2 cups almond meal

1 teaspoon ground cinnamon

1. Heat the banana in a small saucepan over medium heat, stirring frequently.

2. While the banana is heating, whisk the eggs, almond milk, and vanilla together in a small bowl. Add the egg mixture to the banana and stir to mix.

3. Slowly stir in the almond meal and cinnamon. Cover, reduce the heat to low, and let simmer, stirring occasionally, for about 5 minutes, until the mixture is thick and hot. Serve immediately.

Red Pepper, Spinach, and Goat Cheese Frittata Bites

SERVES 8 (MAKES 24 BITES)   PREP TIME: 10 MINUTES   COOK TIME: 10 MINUTES

Eggs are a great protein-filled breakfast food, and these frittata bites, filled with veggies and goat cheese, are delicious. They're lovely for a Sunday brunch, but since they are also good at room temperature, they're a great dish to make ahead and keep around for a speedy breakfast on the run.

Coconut oil for the pan
8 eggs
¼ cup almond milk
½ teaspoon salt
½ teaspoon freshly ground black pepper
3 cups chopped fresh spinach leaves
1 small red bell pepper, seeded and diced small
4 ounces goat cheese, crumbled

1. Preheat the oven to 375°F. Coat a 24-cup mini muffin tin with coconut oil.

2. In a large bowl, whisk together the eggs, almond milk, salt, and pepper. Stir in the spinach, bell pepper, and cheese.

3. Spoon the egg mixture into the prepared muffin tin, filling each cup almost to the top. Bake for 8 to 10 minutes, until puffed and set in the center. Transfer the bites to a serving platter and serve immediately.

4. Store extra bites in an airtight container in the refrigerator for up to 5 days, or freeze them for up to 3 months. Bring to room temperature before serving.

Poached Eggs with Asparagus

SERVES 4 PREP TIME: 5 MINUTES COOK TIME: 15 MINUTES

Fresh spring asparagus seems to turn any meal into a special occasion, so celebrate the morning with this simple but satisfying breakfast of poached eggs atop broiled asparagus. If asparagus isn't in season, substitute red bell peppers cut into strips or zucchini cut into sticks, and adjust the cooking time as needed. Make sure any accompanying bread you choose consists of 100 percent whole grains.

   1 pound asparagus, trimmed
   2 tablespoons olive oil
   ½ teaspoon salt, plus more for garnish
   ½ teaspoon freshly ground black pepper, plus more for garnish
   8 eggs

1. Preheat the broiler. Set a skillet of water over medium-high heat and bring to a simmer.

2. Meanwhile, arrange the asparagus on a large baking sheet, drizzle with the oil, and sprinkle with the salt and pepper. Broil in the preheated oven for about 5 minutes, flip over, and broil for 3 to 5 minutes, until browned and just tender.

3. When the water in the skillet has come to a simmer, crack each egg first in a cup, then slide it into the water. Reduce the heat to medium-low and simmer for 4 minutes, until the whites are set and the yolks are still runny.

4. Arrange the asparagus equally on 4 serving plates. Top each with 2 eggs and a sprinkling of salt and pepper. Serve immediately.

TIP   The key to perfectly poached eggs is to slide the raw eggs gently into simmering, not boiling, water, then immediately reduce the heat to low to keep the water at a steady simmer—do not let the water boil once the eggs are in. Add the eggs into the water starting at 12 o'clock and move clockwise. Set a timer for 4 minutes and remove the eggs promptly using a slotted spoon, starting with the one at 12 o'clock and moving clockwise.

Smoked Salmon and Egg Sushi

SERVES 4   PREP TIME: I5 MINUTES   COOK TIME: 5 MINUTES

● ● ●   *This breakfast sushi uses scrambled eggs in place of the usual white rice (seasoned with sugar!) and smoked salmon in place of raw fish. Served with coconut aminos instead of soy sauce and a dollop of wasabi paste, this dish will satisfy your sushi cravings. It makes a beautiful breakfast or brunch dish and could also serve as a tasty take-along lunch for work, school, or a picnic.*

5 eggs
½ teaspoon salt
1 tablespoon coconut oil
4 sheets nori (seaweed)
2 ounces thinly sliced smoked salmon (lox)
1½ avocados, sliced
1 cup fresh spinach
1 tablespoon fresh dill, chopped
Wasabi paste, for serving (optional)
Coconut aminos, for serving (optional)

1. In a small bowl, whisk together the eggs and salt.

2. Heat the coconut oil in a medium skillet over medium heat. Add the eggs and cook, stirring frequently, for 3 to 4 minutes, until set. Set aside to cool.

3. Place a small bowl of water next to your work surface.

4. Place a nori sheet on top of either a bamboo sushi mat or a square of plastic wrap.

5. Spoon one-quarter of the cooled eggs along one edge of the nori, leaving about ½ inch clear on the edge to allow you to seal the nori once you've rolled it up. Lay a slice of smoked salmon on top of the egg, then add a layer of avocado and a layer of spinach. Top with the dill. Using the bamboo mat or plastic wrap to help, roll up the nori gently but tightly over the fillings. Dip your finger in the bowl of water, run it along the edge of the nori, and press down to seal the roll. Repeat with the remaining nori sheets and fillings.

6. Using a very sharp knife, slice each roll in half crosswise. Cut each half in half again crosswise to make 4 pieces out of each roll.

7. Serve immediately with wasabi paste and coconut aminos for dipping, if desired.

TIP   Nori is the thin, toasted seaweed that is used to wrap sushi rolls. It is sold in packs of 10 or more sheets and can be found in the Asian foods section of many supermarkets, at Asian food markets, or online.

Eggs Benedict

Runny poached eggs, salty and meaty Canadian bacon, and rich hollandaise sauce combine to make a most decadent breakfast. Making hollandaise sauce in the blender is pretty much foolproof and gets this dish on the table in no time. If desired, you could add a bit of sautéed or steamed spinach for greenery.

12 slices Canadian bacon

10 tablespoons unsalted butter

3 egg yolks

1 tablespoon freshly squeezed lemon juice

½ teaspoon salt

Pinch of cayenne pepper or dash of hot pepper sauce (optional)

6 eggs

2 tablespoons chopped fresh parsley, for garnish

1. Heat a large skillet over medium heat. Add the Canadian bacon. Cook for 2 to 3 minutes, until lightly browned, then flip over and cook the other side for 2 to 3 minutes, until lightly browned. Transfer 2 slices of bacon to each of 6 serving plates.

2. Meanwhile, fill a large saucepan with water to a depth of 4 inches and bring to a boil. Reduce the heat to low to maintain a gentle simmer.

3. To make the hollandaise sauce, melt the butter and set aside. Place the egg yolks, lemon juice, salt, and cayenne pepper or hot pepper sauce, if using, in a blender, and process for about 30 seconds, until the mixture is pale yellow. With the blender running on low speed, slowly drizzle the melted butter into the egg mixture for about 1 minute, until the mixture is thick and well combined.

4. Meanwhile, crack each egg first in a cup, then slide it into the water. Simmer for 4 minutes, until the whites are set and the yolks are still runny.

5. Top the Canadian bacon on each plate with one poached egg and drizzle with the sauce. Serve immediately, garnished with parsley.

Prosciutto and Eggs Baked in Mushroom Caps

SERVES 4   PREP TIME: 5 MINUTES   COOK TIME: 20 MINUTES

● ● ●   *Known for its delicate texture and rich flavor, prosciutto is the star of this recipe, lining mushroom cap bowls that serve as edible plates for herbed eggs. This is impressive enough to serve guests for Sunday brunch, but it's quick and simple enough to make any day of the week. If you don't want to splurge on prosciutto, use thinly sliced ham instead.*

4 portobello mushroom caps

1 tablespoon olive oil

4 slices prosciutto

4 eggs

1 teaspoon minced fresh thyme

¼ teaspoon salt

¼ teaspoon freshly ground black pepper

1. Preheat the oven to 350°F. Line a baking sheet with parchment paper.

2. Remove the stems from the mushroom caps and scrape out the gills to make a smooth bowl. Brush the outside of each mushroom cap with oil and arrange them in a single layer, upside down, on the prepared baking sheet.

3. Line each mushroom with a slice of prosciutto, then crack an egg into it. Sprinkle the tops with the thyme, salt, and pepper. Bake for about 20 minutes, until the eggs are set and the mushrooms are soft.

Vietnamese-Style Omelet

SERVES I   PREP TIME: 5 MINUTES   COOK TIME: 3 MINUTES

● ● ●   *This simple omelet gets complex flavor from the fish sauce and bright notes from fresh cilantro and scallion. It takes only minutes to prepare and makes a fantastic breakfast, or served alongside a green salad or roasted veggies, a perfect light lunch or dinner.*

2 eggs

½ teaspoon fish sauce

1 tablespoon chopped fresh cilantro, plus more for garnish

1 scallion, thinly sliced, plus more for garnish

1 squeeze of fresh lime juice

1 tablespoon coconut oil

1. Whisk the eggs in a small bowl until lightly beaten. Add the fish sauce, cilantro, scallion, and lime juice, and whisk to combine.

2. Heat the coconut oil in a medium skillet over medium heat. Add the egg mixture and cook for about 1 minute, until the egg begins to set. When the egg has set on the bottom and around the edges, begin pushing the outer edges toward the center with a spatula and tilting the pan to let the uncooked egg run around the edges. Continue in this manner for about 2 minutes, until the egg is set but not dry. Fold the omelet over and slide onto a serving plate. Serve immediately, garnished with additional cilantro and scallion.

Eggs Baked in Avocados

Creamy avocado gets even more delectable when heated. Filled with a perfectly baked egg, half an avocado makes an ideal edible bowl. This breakfast is full with protein, omega-3 fatty acids, and fiber, making it a nutritious way to start your day. If you like, top the eggs with a spoonful or two of salsa.

2 ripe avocados, halved and pitted

4 eggs

¼ teaspoon salt

⅛ teaspoon freshly ground black pepper

1 tablespoon chopped chives (optional)

1. Preheat the oven to 425°F.

2. Hollow out each avocado half by scooping out about 2 tablespoons of the flesh. (Reserve for another use.) Put the avocado halves, cut-side up, in a baking dish.

3. Crack the eggs, one at a time, into the avocado halves. Bake in the preheated oven for 15 to 20 minutes, until the whites are set but the yolks are still a bit runny. Serve immediately, garnished with salt, pepper, and chives (if using).

TIP   Use up the extra avocado to replace the avocado called for in Chipotle Guacamole (see page 162). Toss it in lemon juice to keep it bright green and make the guacamole on the same day.

Eggs Baked in a Bacon Crust

SERVES 8   PREP TIME: 5 MINUTES   COOK TIME: 25 MINUTES

● ● ●   *There's nothing like bacon and eggs to get a day started right. These cute individual quiches replace the usual pastry crust with crisp bacon for a perfect on-the-go breakfast. Filled with mushrooms and greens, they are hearty and satisfying. Their mess-free preparation makes them great for serving a crowd or making extra for ready-to-serve breakfasts for subsequent days. Leftovers can be reheated in the microwave.*

8 strips bacon
1 tablespoon olive oil
1 small onion, chopped
¾ cup chopped fresh button or cremini mushrooms
1 pound fresh Swiss chard, stemmed and cut into ribbons
8 eggs
¾ teaspoon salt
¼ teaspoon freshly ground black pepper

1. Preheat the oven to 350° F.

2. Wrap 1 strip of bacon in each cup of an 8-cup muffin tin to form a continuous band around the inside perimeter.

3. Heat the oil in a medium skillet over medium-high heat. Add the onion and mushrooms and cook, stirring, for about 3 minutes, until they begin to soften. Add the chard and cook for 3 to 4 minutes, until wilted.

4. Whisk the eggs to beat and add the salt and pepper. Stir the vegetable mixture into the eggs, then ladle equally into the bacon-lined muffin cups.

5. Bake for about 30 minutes, until puffed and golden. Serve immediately or cool to room temperature. Store in the fridge for up to 5 days or in the freezer for up to 3 months.

TIP   If you are on the yellow or green plan, you may add ½ cup shredded cheese (try Cheddar or Gruyère) to the egg mixture.

Crispy Cauliflower Pancakes

SERVES 4 PREP TIME: 10 MINUTES COOK TIME: 6 MINUTES

These veggie-filled, grain-free, dairy-free pancakes make for a easy and delicious meal. Full of both protein and fiber, they'll keep you feeling satisfied all morning long. These pancakes reheat nicely in the microwave, so make extra and stash a few in the fridge for another day.

1 large head cauliflower, cut into small florets

2 medium carrots, grated

4 eggs

½ cup almond meal

½ cup raw, unsalted sunflower seeds

½ cup hazelnuts, finely chopped

½ cup fresh parsley, finely chopped

2 teaspoons freshly squeezed lime juice

1 teaspoon salt

½ teaspoon freshly ground black pepper

2 teaspoons fresh thyme

1 teaspoon smoked paprika

½ teaspoon cayenne pepper

2 tablespoons olive oil, plus more as needed

1. Place the cauliflower in a food processor or blender and pulse until it resembles a coarse meal. Transfer to a large mixing bowl.

2. Add the carrots, eggs, almond meal, sunflower seeds, hazelnuts, parsley, lime juice, salt, black pepper, thyme, paprika, and cayenne pepper, and mix to combine well.

3. Heat the oil in a medium nonstick skillet over medium-high heat. Spoon the batter into the pan about ¼ cup at a time. Flatten each round quickly with the back of the ladle.

4. Cook for about 3 minutes per side, until the pancakes are golden brown. Repeat until you have used up all the batter, adding a bit more oil between batches if needed.

5. Serve immediately.

Homemade Breakfast Sausage Patties

● ● ●   *Store-bought breakfast sausage is often loaded with sugar (not to mention some of the other questionable ingredients). This version consists only of meat and spices, exactly as a good breakfast sausage should. Serve it by itself or alongside whatever style of eggs you prefer.*

- 1 pound ground pork
- 1 teaspoon salt
- 1 teaspoon dried sage
- 1 teaspoon dried thyme
- 1 teaspoon paprika
- 1 teaspoon freshly ground black pepper
- ½ teaspoon cayenne pepper
- ¼ teaspoon ground nutmeg

1. Preheat the oven to 350°F.

2. In a large bowl, add the pork and all the spices, and mix well with your hands.

3. Form the meat mixture into 12 balls, and place each into the cup of a 12-cup muffin tin, flattening them into a patty.

4. Bake for 20 to 25 minutes, until cooked through and lightly browned on the outside.

5. Serve hot.

TIP   Wrap leftovers tightly in plastic wrap, and store in the refrigerator for up to 3 days or in the freezer for up to 3 months.

Spicy Scrambled Eggs with Sausage

SERVES 4   PREP TIME: 5 MINUTES   COOK TIME: 10 MINUTES

● ● ● *A hearty scramble is a great breakfast to make for a crowd in a hurry. Studded with bits of sausage, juicy tomatoes, spicy chiles, and bright bell pepper, this one is like a fiesta on a plate. Full of protein, veggies, and healthy fat, it will get you off on the right foot and keep you going until lunch.*

8 eggs
¾ teaspoon salt
½ teaspoon freshly ground pepper
½ teaspoon dried oregano
½ teaspoon paprika
2 teaspoons coconut oil
2 fresh sausage links (chicken or pork, mild or spicy), with casings removed, crumbled
1 zucchini, diced
1 large red or orange bell pepper, seeded and diced
1 medium tomato, seeded and diced
1 jalapeño chile, seeded and diced
¼ cup chopped fresh cilantro

1. Whisk together the eggs, salt, pepper, oregano, and paprika in a medium bowl.

2. Heat the oil in a large skillet over medium-high heat. Add the sausage, zucchini, bell pepper, tomato, and jalapeño chile, and cook, stirring frequently, for 5 minutes, until the sausage is browned and the vegetables have softened.

3. Stir in the egg mixture and continue to cook, stirring continuously, for 5 minutes, or until the eggs are set. Garnish with cilantro. Serve hot.

Jack Cheese Omelet with Peppers and Chives

SERVES 2 PREP TIME: 5 MINUTES COOK TIME: 10 MINUTES

Omelets provide a perfect way to make simple ingredients into an elegant meal without a lot of fuss. Here delicately cooked eggs are filled with creamy Monterey Jack cheese, bright bell peppers, and chives for a satisfying breakfast. If you like, add a dollop of spicy salsa or hot sauce.

1 teaspoon coconut oil

½ red bell pepper, diced

½ yellow bell pepper, diced

4 eggs, beaten

¼ teaspoon salt

¼ teaspoon freshly ground black pepper

2 ounces sliced Monterey Jack cheese

2 tablespoons chopped fresh chives

1. Heat the coconut oil in a medium nonstick skillet over medium heat.

2. Combine the red and yellow peppers in a bowl, and mix to combine.

3. In a medium bowl, whisk the eggs with the salt and pepper. To make the first omelet, pour half of the eggs to the pan, and cook until the edges begin to set. Using a spatula, push the set edges toward the center of the pan, and tilt the pan to let the uncooked egg fill in around the rim.

4. When the eggs are nearly set, cover half of the omelet with half of the red and yellow pepper filling, followed by half of the cheese. Cook for 1 minute, until the cheese begins to melt. Sprinkle the chives over the cheese and fold the omelets in half over the filling.

5. Slide the omelet onto a serving plate. Repeat to make the second omelet. Serve immediately.

Fluffy Bacon and Chive Egg Puffs

SERVES 4   PREP TIME: 5 MINUTES   COOK TIME: 6 MINUTES

Made of egg whites and cheese, and studded with bacon bits and chives, these puffs could be described as rustic soufflés or as fluffy, savory clouds. The perfectly runny yolk is a rich, flavorful treasure in the center.

2 strips bacon

4 eggs

¼ cup grated Parmesan cheese

¼ cup chopped chives

½ teaspoon salt, plus more for sprinkling on the yolk

¼ teaspoon freshly ground black pepper, plus more for sprinkling on the yolk

1. Preheat the oven to 450°F. Line a baking sheet with parchment paper.

2. Cook the bacon in a medium skillet over medium-high heat for about 4 minutes per side, until browned and crisp. Drain on paper towels and crumble.

3. Separate the eggs, putting the whites in a large bowl and putting the 4 yolks into 4 separate small bowls.

4. Beat the egg whites until they form stiff peaks. Add the bacon, Parmesan cheese, chives, salt, and pepper, and fold in gently until just combined. Scoop the batter onto the prepared baking sheet in 4 equal mounds, and create a well in the center of each mound.

5. Bake for 3 minutes. Remove from the oven, drop one yolk into each well, sprinkle with salt and pepper, and return to the oven to bake for about 3 minutes, until the yolks are just set. Serve immediately.

Mexican Quiche Baked in Bell Peppers

SERVES 6   PREP TIME: 10 MINUTES   COOK TIME: 45 MINUTES

Brightly colored bell peppers (choose orange, red, yellow, green, or a combination of colors) make tasty edible cooking vessels for a simple quiche filling, while spicy chorizo adds flavor and extra protein. If you can't find chorizo, feel free to substitute another spicy sausage.

3 bell peppers, tops removed and seeded

½ pound Mexican chorizo sausage

½ small onion, chopped

2 garlic cloves, minced

6 eggs

¼ cup whole milk

½ cup shredded whole-milk mozzarella cheese

¾ teaspoon salt

½ teaspoon freshly ground black pepper

1. Preheat the oven to 350°F.

2. Set the bell peppers in a baking dish, cut-side up.

3. Heat a large skillet over medium-high heat. Add the sausage and cook, stirring and breaking it up with a spatula, for about 4 minutes, until it starts to brown. Add the onion and garlic, and continue to cook, stirring, for about 3 minutes, until the vegetables begin to soften. Remove from the heat and set aside to cool.

4. In a medium bowl, whisk together the eggs, milk, cheese, salt, and pepper. Stir in the cooked chorizo mixture and mix well.

5. Spoon the egg mixture into the peppers, dividing equally. Bake for 35 to 40 minutes, until the eggs are completely set. Serve hot.

Sausage-Crusted Quiche with Swiss Chard

SERVES I2   PREP TIME: I0 MINUTES   COOK TIME: 40 MINUTES

Using sausage to make a grain-free crust is just brilliant. Full of flavor and protein, it makes an ideal holder for a creamy egg mixture enriched with ricotta cheese and laced with sautéed onions and chard. These quiches are quite filling, and they're portable, too.

1 tablespoon coconut oil

1 small onion, chopped

1 garlic clove, minced

8 cups Swiss chard, chopped

⅛ teaspoon ground nutmeg

½ teaspoon salt

¼ teaspoon freshly ground black pepper

1 pound mild ground pork sausage

5 eggs

2 cups whole-milk ricotta cheese

1. Preheat the oven to 350°F.

2. Heat the coconut oil in a large skillet over medium-high heat. Add the onion and garlic and cook, stirring, for about 5 minutes, until softened. Add the chard and cook, stirring frequently, about 5 minutes, until the leaves have wilted and the stems are soft. Stir in the nutmeg, salt, and pepper to combine well, and remove from the heat.

3. Press the sausage into the cups of a 12-cup muffin tin, pressing to create a ¼-inch-thick layer on the bottom and up sides of each cup.

4. In a large bowl, beat the eggs. Add the ricotta and the cooled chard mixture and stir to combine well. Spoon the filling equally into the sausage shells.

5. Place the filled muffin tin on top of a baking sheet, and bake for 25 to 30 minutes, until the egg mixture is puffed, golden, and set in the middle. Serve immediately.

TIP   The quiches can be stored in the refrigerator for up to 3 days or in the freezer for up to 3 months. Cool them completely before wrapping in plastic wrap and storing.

Quick Butternut Squash and Sausage Hash

SERVES 4   PREP TIME: 10 MINUTES   COOK TIME: 20 MINUTES

● ● ●   *Who needs toast when you've got a plate of this delicious and colorful—not to mention super nutritious—hash to complement your eggs? Butternut squash adds bright color and a rich, slightly sweet flavor to this spicy hash. Be sure to check the sausage ingredients to make sure there are no added sweeteners. Serve the hash topped with fried or poached eggs, if you like.*

2 hot or mild Italian sausage links, casings removed

2 garlic cloves, minced

2 cups diced butternut squash

½ medium yellow onion, diced

¾ teaspoon salt

½ teaspoon freshly ground black pepper

1 medium red, yellow, or green bell pepper, seeded and diced

1 medium tomato, finely chopped

2 cups fresh spinach leaves

1. Heat a large skillet over medium heat. Add the sausage and cook for about 5 minutes, until browned, stirring frequently and breaking up the chunks with a wooden spoon. Add the garlic and cook, stirring, for 1 minute.

2. Stir in the squash, onion, salt, and pepper. Continue to cook, stirring frequently, for 5 minutes. Add the diced bell pepper and cook, stirring occasionally, for 5 minutes. Add the chopped tomato and cook, stirring occasionally, for 5 minutes.

3. Stir in the spinach and cook for 2 to 3 minutes, until wilted. Serve immediately.

> **TIP** You can often find diced butternut squash prepared in bags in the fresh produce section or freezer section of your supermarket. If you are starting with a whole squash, microwave it for 6 to 8 minutes before peeling and cutting to make the task significantly easier.

Spicy Asian Shrimp Salad with Jicama

SERVES 4   PREP TIME: 10 MINUTES   COOK TIME: NONE

Cooked shrimp offer an excellent option for adding protein to a light salad. With crunchy carrots, crisp jicama, fresh herbs, chiles, and a tangy lime dressing, this salad is very satisfying yet light enough for a warm summer day.

1 large jicama, peeled and julienned

1 large carrot, peeled and julienned

2 stalks celery, finely sliced

¼ cup chopped fresh mint

¼ cup chopped fresh cilantro

2 serrano chiles, seeded and minced

½ pound peeled, cooked medium shrimp, halved lengthwise

6 tablespoons freshly squeezed lime juice

2 tablespoons fish sauce

1 tablespoon olive oil

⅓ cup chopped almonds, for garnish

1. In a large bowl, toss together the jicama, carrot, celery, mint, cilantro, and chiles. Add the shrimp and toss to combine.

2. In a small bowl, whisk together the lime juice, fish sauce, and olive oil. Pour the mixture over the vegetables and shrimp, and toss well to coat. Serve immediately, garnished with chopped almonds.

Avocado and Vegetable Sushi

SERVES 4   PREP TIME: 15 MINUTES   COOK TIME: NONE

Filled with creamy avocado, crisp vegetables, and a secret sauce, these sushi rolls make a fantastic vegetarian lunch. If desired, add flaked smoked salmon, poached shrimp, grilled salmon, or another protein. These rolls make a handy portable lunch to take to work or school or on a picnic.

¼ cup tablespoons nutritional yeast

2 tablespoons Dijon mustard

4 teaspoons coconut aminos

2 tablespoons freshly squeezed lemon or lime juice

1 tablespoon chopped fresh cilantro

Salt

Freshly ground black pepper

8 nori (seaweed) sheets

2 avocados, mashed

1 red bell pepper, seeded and cut into thin strips

1 large carrot, cut into thin strips

1 medium zucchini, cut into thin strips

2 cups sprouts (such as alfalfa)

1. To make the secret sauce, add the nutritional yeast, mustard, coconut aminos, lemon juice, and cilantro in a small bowl, and stir to mix well. Season with salt and pepper.

2. To assemble the sushi, place a small bowl of water next to your work surface and place 1 nori sheet on top of either a bamboo sushi mat or a square of plastic wrap. ▶

3. Spread some of the sauce on the half of the nori sheet closest to you (leaving about ½ inch on the end to allow you to seal the nori once you've rolled it up.). Spoon a quarter of the avocado over the sauce. Top with one-quarter each of the bell pepper, carrot, zucchini, and sprouts. Using the bamboo mat or plastic wrap to help, gently but tightly roll up the nori over the filling. When you reach the end, dip your finger in the bowl of water and run it along the edge of the nori, then press it down to seal the roll. Repeat with the remaining nori sheets and fillings.

4. Using a very sharp knife, slice each roll in half crosswise. Cut each half crosswise in half again to make 4 pieces.

5. Serve immediately with the remaining sauce for dipping, if desired.

TIP   The nutritional yeast used in the sauce can be found in any health food or natural foods store. It contributes umami flavor similar to what you'd get from soy sauce.

Seared Tuna Salad

SERVES 4   PREP TIME: 5 MINUTES   COOK TIME: 2 MINUTES

A seared tuna salad is elegant and satisfying, and extremely simple to make. The key to succulent tuna is not to overcook it: the surface of the fish should be lightly browned, while the center should remain pink and succulent.

2 tablespoons coconut aminos

2 tablespoons rice vinegar

1 tablespoon olive oil, plus 1 tablespoon

1 small cucumber, halved lengthwise and thinly sliced

1 pound fresh, sushi-grade ahi tuna steak

Salt

Freshly ground black pepper

4 cups mixed greens

1. In a large bowl, whisk together the coconut aminos, vinegar, and 1 tablespoon of olive oil. Add the cucumber slices and toss to coat.

2. Heat the remaining 1 tablespoon of olive oil in a large skillet over medium-high heat. Season the tuna on both sides with salt and pepper, and add it to the pan. Reduce the heat to medium and cook for about 1 minute, until browned on the bottom. Flip it over and cook for about 1 minute, until the other side is browned (the middle should still be essentially raw).

3. Transfer the tuna to a cutting board and slice against the grain into ½-inch-thick slices.

4. To serve, divide the greens evenly among 4 serving plates. Top each with one-quarter of the tuna and one-quarter of the cucumbers. Drizzle the remaining vinaigrette over the fish and serve immediately.

TIP   Because the fish isn't cooked all the way through, it's important to use only sushi-grade tuna.

Grain-Free Falafel Patties
with Zucchini

SERVES 4   PREP TIME: I0 MINUTES   COOK TIME: I5 MINUTES

● ● ●   *This flavorful falafel uses almond meal in place of chickpeas for a low-carbohydrate version of a favorite vegetarian dish. Serve the patties over a mixed green salad with Tahini Lemon Dressing (page 361), or wrap them in lettuce leaves for a falafel wrap.*

¾ cup almond meal

½ onion, diced

1 cup grated zucchini (about 1 medium squash)

2 garlic cloves, minced

1 tablespoon chopped fresh parsley

2 tablespoons chopped fresh cilantro

1 teaspoon baking soda

1 teaspoon ground cumin

½ teaspoon cayenne pepper

2 teaspoons ground coriander

½ teaspoon salt

½ teaspoon freshly ground black pepper

3 tablespoons olive oil

1. In the bowl of a food processor or blender, mix all of the ingredients except for the olive oil, and pulse until well blended.

2. Form the mixture into 1-inch balls, flatten the balls into patties about 1½ inches in diameter, and place the patties on a baking sheet.

3. Refrigerate the patties for at least 30 minutes.

4. Heat the olive oil in a large skillet over medium heat. Add the patties in a single layer (you'll need to cook them in batches), and cook for about 3 minutes, until golden brown on the bottom. Turn the patties over and cook for about 3 minutes, until the other side is golden brown. Drain on paper towels and serve hot.

Lemon-Lime Shrimp Ceviche with Avocado

SERVES 4
PREP TIME: 15 MINUTES (PLUS 90 MINUTES FOR CHILLING AND MARINATING)
COOK TIME: 3 MINUTES

● ● ● *Ceviche is traditionally made by marinating raw seafood in an acidic liquid, such as lime juice, for several hours, which effectively "cooks" the seafood. This recipe calls for pre-poaching the shrimp, which cuts hours off the preparation time. The shrimp turn out plump and sweet, with a hit of spice.*

2 quarts water
¼ cup salt, plus ¼ teaspoon
1 pound peeled and deveined shrimp
Juice of 2 lemons
Juice of 2 limes
1 tablespoon red wine vinegar
2 serrano chiles, seeded and finely diced
1 large tomato, seeded and diced
1 avocado, diced
1 tablespoon chopped fresh cilantro, plus more for garnish
¼ cup olive oil

1. In a large saucepan, add the water and ¼ cup of salt, and bring to a boil over high heat. Drop the shrimp into the boiling water, then remove the saucepan from the heat. Let the shrimp sit in the water for about 3 minutes, until just cooked through. Drain and set aside until cool enough to handle. Chop the shrimp into ½-inch pieces.

2. In a medium, nonreactive (glass or ceramic) bowl, add the shrimp, lemon juice, lime juice, vinegar, and chiles, toss to combine, and refrigerate for 1 hour.

3. In a large nonreactive bowl, add the tomato, avocado, cilantro, olive oil, and the remaining ¼ teaspoon of salt, and stir to combine. Add the shrimp mixture, stir, and let it stand at room temperature for 30 minutes before serving.

Fresh Herb Frittata with Peas, Bacon, and Feta Cheese

SERVES 8   PREP TIME: 5 MINUTES   COOK TIME: 20 MINUTES

A frittata is quick to make and endlessly versatile—it's delicious served hot or warm, or at room temperature as well, so it also makes for a convenient take-along lunch. This version combines fresh mint with bright green peas, salty bacon, and tangy goat cheese. If you can find fresh peas, by all means use them, but frozen peas are perfectly acceptable for this dish.

1 tablespoon olive oil

½ small onion, diced

1 garlic clove, minced

4 strips bacon, diced

2 cups frozen peas, thawed

10 eggs

2 tablespoons almond milk

¾ teaspoon salt

½ cup (2 ounces) crumbled goat cheese, plus ½ cup

2 tablespoons chopped fresh mint

1. Preheat the oven to 450°F.

2. Heat the olive oil in a large oven-safe skillet over medium-high heat. Add the onion, garlic, and bacon, and cook, stirring frequently, for about 5 minutes, until the onion is soft and the bacon is crisp. Stir in the peas and cook for 2 minutes.

3. In a medium bowl, whisk the eggs with the almond milk and salt. Add 2 ounces of the cheese to the eggs along with the mint, and whisk to combine. Pour the egg mixture over the vegetables in the skillet. Place the skillet in the oven and cook for 8 to 10 minutes, until the top is nearly set.

4. Crumble the remaining 2 ounces of goat cheese over the top. Set the broiler to high and place the skillet under it. Broil for about 3 minutes, until the cheese turns golden brown. Serve immediately or let cool to room temperature.

5. To store leftovers, cut the frittata into wedges and wrap individually in plastic wrap. Refrigerate for up to 3 days or freeze for up to 3 months. Bring to room temperature before serving.

Roasted Brussels Sprout Salad with Crumbled Bacon

SERVES 4   PREP TIME: I0 MINUTES   COOK TIME: 20 MINUTES

● ● ●   *The surprising combination of roasted Brussels sprouts, crisp bacon, crunchy apples, and fresh mint makes a wonderful salad. This salad keeps well, so it makes a great lunch to bring along to work as well as a tasty side dish at dinner with grilled or roasted meat or fish.*

3 cups Brussels sprouts, trimmed and halved
1 tablespoon olive oil, plus 1 tablespoon, plus more for drizzling
½ teaspoon salt
¼ teaspoon freshly ground black pepper
4 strips bacon
1 green apple, cored and thinly sliced
2 tablespoons torn fresh mint leaves
1 tablespoon freshly squeezed lemon juice

1. Preheat the oven to 425°F.

2. Place the sprouts on a large rimmed baking sheet and toss with 1 tablespoon olive oil and the salt and pepper. Roast, stirring once or twice, for about 20 minutes, until the sprouts begin to turn golden brown and crispy around the edges. Remove from the oven and let cool.

3. Meanwhile, cook the bacon in a medium skillet over medium-high heat for about 4 minutes per side, until crisp. Drain on paper towels and crumble. ▶

4. In a large bowl, toss together the apple, mint, lemon juice, roasted sprouts, and remaining 1 tablespoon of olive oil. Serve sprinkled with the crumbled bacon.

> TIP   This salad can be made up to 2 days ahead, but the bacon should be cooked just before serving to keep it crisp and the mint should be added before serving to keep it fresh. Store the salad in the refrigerator, and bring it to room temperature before serving.

Spinach Salad with Chicken in a Sun-Dried Tomato and Basil Vinaigrette

SERVES 4   PREP TIME: 10 MINUTES   COOK TIME: NONE

This simple salad provides a great solution for turning leftover roasted chicken into a hearty and satisfying lunch. The sweet-yet-tart dressing uses balsamic vinegar and gets intense flavor from sun-dried tomatoes and a handful of chopped fresh basil.

½ cup Balsamic Vinaigrette (page 360)

2 halves sun-dried tomato (packed in oil, drained), minced

1 tablespoon minced fresh basil

6 cups fresh spinach leaves

1 cup cherry tomatoes

12 ounces shredded chicken breast

1. In a small bowl, whisk together the vinaigrette, sun-dried tomatoes, and fresh basil.

2. In a large bowl, toss together the spinach and tomatoes.

3. Add the chicken and the dressing, and toss to coat. Serve immediately, or store, covered for up to 6 hours, in the refrigerator until ready to eat. If you wish to store the salad longer, keep the spinach and cherry tomatoes, the chicken, and the dressing in separate containers in the fridge, and toss together just before serving.

Curried Chicken Salad Lettuce Wraps with Homemade Mayonnaise

SERVES 4   PREP TIME: 10 MINUTES   COOK TIME: NONE

Curry powder gives this quick chicken salad a spicy kick, while chunks of crisp apple temper the heat with just a hint of sweetness and add a nice textural contrast. This chicken salad is made with a quick Homemade Mayonnaise.

2½ cups (about 12 ounces) chopped cooked chicken breast

1 large green apple, cored and diced

½ cup Homemade Mayonnaise (recipe page 364)

1 tablespoon curry powder

¾ teaspoon salt

½ teaspoon freshly ground black pepper

4 large lettuce leaves, such as Bibb or butter lettuce

1. In a medium bowl, add the chicken and apple and stir to combine. Add the mayonnaise, curry powder, salt, and pepper, and stir to mix well. Taste and adjust seasoning as needed.

2. Arrange the 4 lettuce leaves on your work surface, and divide the chicken mixture evenly among them, piling the mixture down the center of each leaf. Wrap the lettuce up around the filling like a burrito. Wrap well in plastic wrap, and store in the fridge until ready to eat for up to 1 day.

Pesto Chicken Salad

SERVES 4   PREP TIME: 10 MINUTES   COOK TIME: NONE

●●● *This healthy green chicken salad puts a refreshing spin on an old classic. If you don't have Fresh Basil Pesto on hand, you can use a store-bought pesto. Just be sure to check for cheese in the ingredients if you are on the blue plan. If you prefer not to make the mayonnaise, simply substitute plain yogurt.*

½ cup Fresh Basil Pesto (page 365)

1 (10-ounce) package frozen chopped spinach, thawed and squeezed dry

1½ tablespoons freshly squeezed lemon juice

½ cup Homemade Mayonnaise (page 364)

1 pound cooked chicken, diced small

¾ teaspoon salt

¾ teaspoon freshly ground black pepper

4 large lettuce leaves, such as Bibb or butter lettuce

1. In the bowl of a food processor or blender, add the Fresh Basil Pesto, spinach, and lemon juice and process until smooth. Add the Homemade Mayonnaise and process for about 10 seconds more, just to combine.

2. In a medium mixing bowl, add the chicken and the pesto mixture, and toss to coat. Add the salt and pepper, and stir to mix well.

3. To serve, place the lettuce leaves on 4 serving plates. Divide the chicken mixture evenly among the lettuce leaves and serve immediately. Leftovers will keep for up to 2 days in the refrigerator.

Cobb Salad

SERVES 4   PREP TIME: 10 MINUTES   COOK TIME: NONE

● ● ●   *This Cobb salad maintains the essential elements of the classic dish, including diced chicken, hard-boiled eggs, crispy bacon, creamy avocado, and a tangy vinaigrette. Of course, blue cheese is one of the quintessential ingredients of a true Cobb salad, and here it's optional for those on the yellow or green plan.*

3 tablespoons white wine vinegar

2 tablespoons finely minced shallot

1 tablespoon Dijon mustard

1 teaspoon freshly ground black pepper

¼ teaspoon salt

3 tablespoons olive oil

10 cups mixed salad greens

8 ounces shredded cooked chicken breast

2 hard-boiled eggs, peeled and chopped

2 medium tomatoes, diced

1 large cucumber, seeded and sliced

1 avocado, diced

2 slices bacon, cooked and crumbled

½ cup crumbled blue cheese (optional)

1. In a small bowl, whisk together the vinegar, shallot, mustard, pepper, and salt. While whisking constantly, drizzle in the oil, and continue to whisk until the dressing is well combined and emulsified.

2. In a large bowl, toss together the salad greens and one-half of the dressing.

3. To serve, divide the dressed greens evenly among 4 serving plates. Compose each of these ingredients on top, dividing equally among the plates: the chicken, egg, tomatoes, cucumber, avocado, bacon, and blue cheese, if using. Drizzle the remaining half of the dressing over each of the salads, and serve immediately.

TIP   If you don't have cooked chicken breast on hand, you can poach a boneless, skinless chicken breast in water. Place the chicken in a medium skillet, cover with water, and add a pinch of salt. Bring the water to a boil. Reduce the heat to low, cover, and simmer for 10 to 15 minutes, until the chicken is cooked through. Set aside to cool, then follow the recipe.

Steak Salad with Chilies, Ginger, and Fresh Basil

SERVES 4   PREP TIME: 5 MINUTES   COOK TIME: 10 MINUTES

Steak salad makes a hearty and satisfying grain-free lunch. Grilling the steak takes only a few minutes. Or if you have leftover steak in the fridge, this salad is a perfect way to enjoy it.

½ cup olive oil

¼ cup white wine vinegar

3 garlic cloves, minced

½ teaspoon salt

¼ teaspoon freshly ground black pepper

1½ pounds flank steak

1 large cucumber, peeled

2 scallions, thinly sliced

1 large bunch basil leaves

1 (1-inch) piece fresh ginger, peeled and minced

2 small red serrano chilies, thinly sliced, for garnish

1. Preheat a grill or grill pan to medium-high heat.

2. In a small bowl, whisk together the oil, vinegar, garlic, salt, and pepper until well combined.

3. Season the steak on both sides with salt and pepper, and place on the grill. Cook for about 5 minutes per side for medium rare (add 1 to 2 minutes per side for a more well done steak). Remove the steak to a cutting board, and let it rest for 5 minutes. ▶

4. While the steak is resting, halve the cucumber lengthwise and scoop out the seeds. Thinly slice the cucumber into half-moons. In a large bowl, toss together the cucumber, scallions, basil, and ginger.

5. Slice the meat thinly against the grain. Add the meat to the salad and toss with enough of the dressing to coat it well. Garnish with the chilies and serve immediately.

Mexican Chicken Salad with Chipotle Avocado Dressing

SERVES 4   PREP TIME: 15 MINUTES   COOK TIME: NONE

Avocado makes a perfect base for a rich and creamy yet dairy-free salad dressing. It offers healthy fats and other nutrients, tastes delicious, and makes a stunning green dressing for a fresh salad. Crisp jicama and radishes add a satisfying crunch, so you won't miss the crispy tortilla shell or tortilla chips.

1 head Romaine lettuce, torn into bite-size pieces

6 radishes, trimmed and thinly sliced

1 red bell pepper, seeded and diced

1 small jicama, peeled and diced

½ small red onion, diced

¾ pound cooked chicken breast, shredded or cut into bite-size pieces

1 garlic clove

1 medium avocado, cubed

¼ cup water

3 tablespoons freshly squeezed lime juice (about 2 medium limes)

3 tablespoons olive oil

¼ teaspoon ground chipotle pepper

1 teaspoon salt

1. In a large salad bowl, toss together the lettuce, radishes, bell pepper, jicama, and red onion. Add the chicken and toss again to combine.

2. To make the dressing, mince the garlic in a food processor or blender. Add the avocado, water, lime juice, olive oil, chipotle pepper, and salt, and process to a smooth purée. If it is too thick to pour, add a bit more water or lime juice.

3. Drizzle the dressing over the salad and toss to coat. Serve immediately.

Cabbage-Wrapped Thai Spring Rolls

SERVES 4   PREP TIME: 15 MINUTES   COOK TIME: 6 MINUTES

● ● ●   *This easy appetizer delivers the bright flavors of Thai spring rolls in a low-carb cabbage leaf. The dipping sauce is a departure from the usual sugar-laden peanut sauce, but rest assured, it is bursting with delicious flavor.*

> 8 large cabbage leaves
> 16 medium shrimp, peeled, steamed, and halved lengthwise (about 4 ounces)
> ½ medium jalapeño (or serrano) chile pepper, seeded and chopped
> ¼ cup finely chopped fresh cilantro
> 1 cup coconut milk
> 1½ tablespoons freshly squeezed lime juice
> 2 teaspoons Thai red curry paste
> ½ teaspoon salt
> 1 medium cucumber, peeled, seeded, and julienned
> 1 large carrot, julienned
> 4 scallions, julienned
> 16 fresh basil leaves
> 16 fresh mint leaves

1. Bring a large pot of water to a boil. Add the cabbage leaves and cook 2 to 3 minutes, until softened. Drain and transfer to a bowl of ice water to stop the cooking.

2. To cook the shrimp, bring a medium saucepan of lightly salted water to a boil over medium-high heat. Add the shrimp, reduce the heat to medium, and simmer until the shrimp are pink and cooked through, 2 to 3 minutes. Drain the shrimp and place in a bowl of ice water to stop cooking.

3. To make the dipping sauce, process the jalapeño chile and the cilantro in a food processor or blender until finely chopped. Add the coconut milk, lime juice, curry paste, and salt, and process to combine.

4. To make the rolls, pat the cabbage leaves dry with a towel and lay them out on the work surface. Pat the shrimp dry. Lay 2 shrimp in a row along the rounded top edge of a cabbage leaf. Add one-quarter of the cucumber, carrot, scallions, basil, and mint. Roll up from the rounded part toward the root end. Repeat with the remaining cabbage leaves and filling.

5. Serve immediately with the dipping sauce, or tightly wrap the rolls in plastic wrap and refrigerate for up to 2 days. The sauce can be stored, covered, in the refrigerator for up to 1 week.

Chipotle Turkey Lettuce Wraps

SERVES 4   PREP TIME: 5 MINUTES   COOK TIME: NONE

● ● ●   *These quick and simple wraps are full of flavor and easy to bring along to work or school. This recipe calls for Homemade Mayonnaise, but you can substitute store-bought mayonnaise as long as the ingredients don't include sugar or other sweeteners, or wheat-based additives.*

½ cup Homemade Mayonnaise (page 364)
¼ to ½ teaspoon ground chipotle pepper
8 large leaves lettuce, such as Bibb or butter lettuce
8 slices turkey
8 slices ham
1 avocado, thinly sliced
½ small red onion, thinly sliced

1. In a small bowl, stir together the Homemade Mayonnaise and chipotle pepper.

2. Stack 2 lettuce leaves and brush with one-quarter of the chipotle mayonnaise. Repeat, to make 4 stacks. Top each stack with 2 slices of turkey, 2 slices of ham, one-quarter of the avocado, and one-quarter of the sliced onion.

3. Roll up the wraps and serve immediately.

TIP   If you're on the yellow or green plan, you might add a slice of sharp Cheddar, Monterey Jack, or pepper Jack cheese to each roll.

Lettuce-Wrapped Beef Tacos

SERVES 4   PREP TIME: 5 MINUTES   COOK TIME: 5 MINUTES

Tacos always are a lunchtime favorite—everyone enjoys a meal you can eat with your hands. This version uses Romaine lettuce leaves, which can fold like a taco shell, in place of tortillas to eliminate grains. Since this recipe contains cheese, it is for those on the yellow or green plans only, but you could easily leave it out (or replace it with Cashew Cheese, page 373) if you are on the blue plan.

1 pound lean ground beef

1 teaspoon chili powder

½ teaspoon ground cumin

½ teaspoon dried oregano

½ teaspoon salt

8 large inner leaves of Romaine lettuce

1 small bell pepper (red, yellow, orange, or green), seeded and diced

1 tomato, seeded and diced

4 ounces shredded Cheddar cheese

½ cup salsa (hot or mild)

1. Heat a medium skillet over medium-high heat. Add the ground beef and cook for about 4 minutes, stirring and breaking up any chunks of meat with a spatula until browned. Stir in the chili powder, cumin, oregano, and salt and cook, stirring, for 1 minute.

2. Place 2 lettuce leaves on each of 4 serving plates. Divide the meat mixture evenly among the lettuce leaves. Top each taco with one-quarter of the diced peppers, tomato, cheese, and salsa. Serve immediately.

Chinese Five-Spice Chicken in Lettuce Cups

SERVES 4 PREP TIME: 5 MINUTES COOK TIME: 15 MINUTES

● ● ● *Chicken (or quail) cooked with hoisin sauce and served in lettuce cups is a classic Chinese dish. This simple, quick version swaps a mixture of Sugar-Free Ketchup, vinegar, ginger, and Chinese five-spice powder for the traditional hoisin sauce, since hoisin is loaded with sugar.*

- 1 garlic clove, minced
- 1 tablespoon white vinegar
- 2 tablespoons Sugar-Free Ketchup (page 366)
- 1 teaspoon sesame oil
- 1 teaspoon freshly grated peeled ginger
- 1 teaspoon Chinese five-spice powder
- 3 tablespoons coconut aminos
- 1 pound boneless, skinless chicken breast, cut into strips
- 2 tablespoons olive oil
- 8 large lettuce leaves, such as Bibb or butter lettuce
- 3 scallions, thinly sliced, for garnish
- 1 large carrot, shredded, for garnish
- 1 to 2 serrano chiles, thinly sliced, for garnish

1. In a large bowl, stir together the garlic, vinegar, Sugar-Free Ketchup, sesame oil, ginger, five-spice powder, and coconut aminos. Add the chicken pieces and stir to coat. Cover and refrigerate for at least 30 minutes.

2. Heat the oil in a large, heavy skillet. Strain the chicken pieces and reserve the marinade. Add the chicken pieces to the skillet in a single layer and cook for about 4 minutes, until browned on the bottom. Turn the chicken pieces over and cook for about 4 minutes, until the chicken is browned and just cooked through. Add the reserved marinade and bring to a simmer. Cook for about 5 minutes, until the sauce has thickened. ▶

3. To serve, place 2 lettuce leaves on each of 4 serving plates. Divide the chicken pieces evenly among the lettuce leaves and spoon some of the sauce over each. Garnish with the scallions, shredded carrot, and chiles and serve immediately.

TIP   Chinese five-spice powder is a spice mixture that usually contains ground fennel seeds, cinnamon, cloves, star anise, and Szechuan peppercorns. You can make your own by combining 2 star anise pods, 1 tablespoon cinnamon, ½ teaspoon each fennel seeds, and either Sichuan peppercorns or black peppercorns, and ¼ teaspoon cloves ground to a powder in a spice grinder.

Ham and Veggie Roll-Ups

SERVES 4   PREP TIME: 10 MINUTES   COOK TIME: NONE

If you're craving a ham sandwich, this bread-free roll-up will do the trick. Get creative if you like, and add pickles—just check the ingredients to make sure they're sugar free—cucumbers, or other veggies, or even sliced cheese (if you're on the yellow or green plan).

2 tablespoons Dijon mustard
12 thick slices deli ham
1 cup shredded lettuce
1 small red bell pepper, seeded, sliced into thin slivers
12 chive leaves

1. Spread the mustard on one side of each slice of ham and lay on the work surface

2. Divide the lettuce and pepper slices evenly on top of the ham slices, arranging them in a strip down the center.

3. Roll the ham up around the filling, wrap a chive around each roll, and tie to secure.

4. Serve immediately or refrigerate for up to 1 day.

Creamy Chicken Soup with Roasted Garlic

SERVES 6   PREP TIME: 10 MINUTES   COOK TIME: 1 HOUR 30 MINUTES

Roasting garlic brings out its natural sweetness. This soup combines the deep, complex flavor of roasted garlic with the bite of fresh garlic in a rich, creamy chicken soup so comforting it will cure whatever ails you.

28 garlic cloves (about 2 heads), cloves separated but
   not peeled
3 tablespoons olive oil
2 tablespoons unsalted butter
1 medium onion, thinly sliced
2 teaspoons minced fresh thyme or ½ teaspoon dried thyme
4 cups chicken broth
1 teaspoon salt
½ teaspoon freshly ground black pepper
½ cup heavy cream
1½ pounds cooked chicken breast, cut into bite-size pieces

1. Preheat the oven to 400°F.

2. Put 20 cloves of garlic on a square of aluminum foil, and drizzle with the olive oil. Crimp the foil closed to form a packet. Place the foil packet directly on the oven rack, and roast in the preheated oven until the garlic is soft and golden brown, 45 to 60 minutes.

3. Remove the garlic from the oven, open the foil packet, and let cool. When cool enough to handle, squeeze the garlic cloves out of their papery skins. Peel the remaining uncooked 8 garlic cloves.

4. Melt the butter in a large saucepan over medium heat. Add the onion and cook, stirring frequently, for about 5 minutes, until softened. ▶

5. Stir in the roasted garlic, fresh garlic, and thyme, and cook 2 to 3 minutes, until fragrant.

6. Increase the heat to medium-high. Add the chicken broth, salt, and pepper, stir to combine, and bring to a boil. Reduce the heat to medium-low, and simmer for about 20 minutes.

7. Using an immersion blender, or a countertop blender (in batches), purée the soup. Add the cream and chicken to the soup in the saucepan, and heat over medium heat until hot. Serve immediately, or cool and store in the refrigerator for up to 1 week.

TIP   Garlic is a nutritional powerhouse, providing cardio-vascular benefits and fighting cancer, bacterial and viral illnesses, and inflammation.

Reuben Roll-Ups

SERVES 4   PREP TIME: 10 MINUTES   COOK TIME: NONE

All the flavors of a classic Reuben sandwich from your favorite deli are here—corned beef, Swiss cheese, and sauerkraut. The only thing missing is the rye bread, but you won't even miss it once you take a bite of this flavorful roll-up dunked in zesty Russian dressing. If you're on the blue plan, simply leave out the cheese. You can use store-bought mayonnaise, provided you buy one without added sugar.

3 tablespoons Homemade Mayonnaise (page 364)

2 tablespoons Sugar-Free Ketchup (page 366) or tomato purée

1 tablespoon olive oil

1 tablespoon white wine vinegar

1 dill pickle, minced

1 teaspoon paprika

½ teaspoon salt

12 slices corned beef

12 slices Swiss cheese

1 cup sauerkraut

1. To make the dressing, in a small bowl, whisk together the Homemade Mayonnaise, Sugar-Free Ketchup, olive oil, vinegar, pickle, paprika, and salt. Divide the dressing evenly among 4 small dipping bowls.

2. To make the roll-ups, on the work surface, place one slice of corned beef and top with one slice of Swiss cheese. Arrange a strip of the sauerkraut down the middle of each stack, dividing the sauerkraut evenly. Roll up and secure with toothpicks, if needed.

3. Serve the roll-ups immediately, along with the dressing for dipping. The roll-ups and dressing can be kept separately in the refrigerator for up to 2 days.

NINE

SNACKS

Crispy Lemon-Rosemary Roasted Chickpeas

MAKES ABOUT 2 CUPS (¼ CUP PER SERVING)
PREP TIME: 5 MINUTES   COOK TIME: 35 MINUTES

Roasted chickpeas make a great high-fiber, high-protein snack. Here they are paired with tangy lemon zest and fragrant rosemary, but this recipe is endlessly flexible—you can substitute just about any flavorings you like. Try them, for instance, with chili powder and lime zest, curry powder, or ground mustard seed.

2 (14-ounce) cans chickpeas, rinsed, drained, and patted dry
2 tablespoons olive oil
Zest of 1 lemon
1 tablespoon chopped fresh rosemary leaves
1 teaspoon garlic powder
¾ teaspoon salt

1. Preheat the oven to 400°F.

2. In a medium bowl, toss the chickpeas with the olive oil, lemon zest, rosemary, garlic powder, and salt.

3. Spread the chickpeas out in a single layer on a large rimmed baking sheet, and roast for about 15 minutes. Stir the chickpeas around, and then continue to roast them for 15 to 20 minutes, until they are lightly browned and crisp. Serve warm or at room temperature.

4. Store leftovers in an airtight container at room temperature for up to 1 week.

Smoky Chili Cashews

MAKES ABOUT 3 CUPS
PREP TIME: 5 MINUTES (PLUS 5 MINUTES TO DRAIN THE CASHEWS)
COOK TIME: 55 MINUTES

Plain roasted cashews are delicious, but you might want to give this spiced version a whirl. With a distinctive smoky flavor from smoked paprika and a hit of chili powder, they're as tasty as any store-bought smoked nuts, but with no added sugar or other forbidden ingredients.

Coconut oil for the pan
1 egg white
1 tablespoon water
3 cups cashews
1 tablespoon salt
1 teaspoon smoked paprika
1 teaspoon ground cumin
½ teaspoon chili powder

1. Preheat the oven to 300°F. Lightly coat a large rimmed baking sheet with coconut oil.

2. In a large bowl, whisk together the egg white and water until foamy. Stir in the cashews and toss to coat. Drain the cashews in a colander for 5 minutes.

3. In a large bowl, stir together the cashews, salt, paprika, cumin, and chili powder, and toss to coat. Spread the mixture in a single layer on the prepared baking sheet, and bake for 15 minutes. Stir the cashew mixture around, and spread out again into an even layer. Reduce the heat to 275°F, and bake for 40 minutes, stirring several times.

4. Remove the pan from the oven, and let the cashews cool for several minutes before breaking the clusters apart. Serve immediately, or cool completely and store in an airtight container at room temperature for up to 2 weeks.

Tamari-Roasted Almonds

SERVES 6 TO 8   PREP TIME: 5 MINUTES   COOK TIME: 7 MINUTES

●　●　● *Almonds are a rich source of omega-3 fatty acids and protein, so if you are looking for a healthy snack, try these savory nuts. Tossed in a rich, salty tamari before roasting, they are absolutely incredible.*

2 cups whole raw almonds
2 tablespoons tamari sauce
1 tablespoon coconut oil, melted

1. Preheat the oven to 350°F.

2. Spread the almonds in a single layer on a large rimmed baking sheet. Roast the almonds for about 15 minutes.

3. Reduce the oven temperature to 300°F.

4. Drizzle the tamari and coconut oil over the almonds and toss to coat well. Return the coated almonds to the oven and roast for about 10 minutes, stirring occasionally, until they have browned. Remove the almonds from the oven and let cool before serving.

5. Store the almonds in an airtight container at room temperature for up to 2 weeks, or in the freezer for up to 3 months.

TIP   Be sure to read the label on your curry powder, because some mixtures contain wheat flour. If you can't find one that's wheat-free, make your own by combining 4 tablespoons ground coriander, 2 tablespoons ground turmeric, 2 tablespoons dry mustard powder, 2 tablespoons chili powder, 1 tablespoon cayenne pepper, 1 tablespoon ground cumin, and 1½ teaspoons ground cardamom.

Cinnamon-Spiced Carrot Fries

SERVES 4   PREP TIME: 5 MINUTES   COOK TIME: 20 MINUTES

● ● ●   *Bright orange and full of beta-carotene, carrot sticks are a big nutritional improvement over regular French fries. Spiced with zingy cinnamon and a dash of cumin, these will have you hooked in no time.*

> 2 large carrots, cut into French-fry-size sticks
> 1 tablespoon olive oil
> ½ teaspoon ground cumin
> ¼ teaspoon ground cinnamon
> ½ teaspoon salt
> ¼ teaspoon freshly ground black pepper

1. Preheat the oven to 425°F. Line a large baking sheet with parchment paper.

2. In a medium bowl, toss together the carrots, olive oil, cumin, cinnamon, salt, and pepper.

3. Spread the carrot sticks out on the prepared baking sheet. Bake for about 20 minutes, turning the carrot sticks once halfway through cooking, until they begin to brown. Serve immediately.

Almond Zucchini Dip

MAKES ABOUT 2 CUPS
PREP TIME: 5 MINUTES (PLUS OVERNIGHT TO SOAK THE ALMONDS)
COOK TIME: NONE

● ● ●　*Containing just a handful of ingredients, this raw dip is full of nutty flavor and nutrients. Serve it with veggie sticks for dipping, or use it as a spread on a lettuce wrap for added flavor.*

2 cups raw almonds, soaked in water overnight

2 large zucchini, chopped

1 garlic clove

Juice of 1 lemon

½ teaspoon salt

½ teaspoon freshly ground black pepper

In the bowl of a food processor or blender, add all the ingredients, and process to a chunky purée.

Barbecue-Flavor Zucchini Chips

SERVES 2   PREP TIME: 10 MINUTES   COOK TIME: 1 HOUR 30 MINUTES

● ● ●   *A quick mix of spices from the pantry turns thinly sliced zucchini into a delicious snack that's every bit as scrumptious as BBQ potato chips. Try using one green zucchini and one yellow zucchini for visual appeal. If you're feeling creative, try using other vegetables as well, such as butternut squash, eggplant, parsnips, or carrots.*

Cooking spray

1½ teaspoons paprika

1 teaspoon ground cumin

¾ teaspoon chili powder

¾ teaspoon salt

½ teaspoon onion powder

½ teaspoon garlic powder

¼ teaspoon freshly ground black pepper

2 medium zucchini, sliced into very thin rounds

1. Preheat the oven to 375°F. Coat 1 to 2 large baking sheets with cooking spray.

2. In a small bowl, add the seasoning mix ingredients and stir to combine.

3. Arrange the zucchini slices in a single layer on the prepared baking sheet, coat the slices lightly with more cooking spray, and sprinkle them with some of the seasoning mixture.

4. Bake the slices for 30 to 45 minutes. Rotate the pan, or if using two pans, switch them around, and continue to bake for another 30 to 45 minutes, until the chips are browned and crisp.

5. Remove the zucchini from the oven and let cool for 5 minutes, then transfer it to a bowl and serve, sprinkling with additional seasoning mix, if desired.

> TIP   A mandoline makes quick work of slicing the zucchini and enables you to get very thin rounds. But if you don't have one, a sharp knife and a bit of patience will work just as well. For best results, slice the zucchini $\frac{1}{16}$-inch thick (the thickness of a nickel).

Cauliflower "Popcorn"

SERVES 4   PREP TIME: 5 MINUTES   COOK TIME: 25 MINUTES

Popcorn is off-limits on the sugar detox diet because it's a grain, but this salty, crunchy, delicious version substitutes cauliflower for corn, and it is equally wonderful. For real movie theater flavor, drizzle melted butter over it (if you're on the yellow or green plan) just before serving.

2 tablespoons olive oil

1 teaspoon salt

1 head cauliflower, cut into small florets

1. Preheat the oven to 425°F. Line a large baking sheet with parchment paper.

2. In a large bowl, add the olive oil and salt, whisk, then add the cauliflower florets and toss thoroughly to coat.

3. Spread the cauliflower out in a single layer on the prepared baking sheet, and bake for about 25 minutes, until golden brown and beginning to crisp.

4. Serve immediately.

Olive Tapenade

MAKES ABOUT 1 CUP   PREP TIME: 10 MINUTES   COOK TIME: NONE

● ● ●   *Olive tapenade is a traditional Mediterranean spread made of olives, capers, garlic, herbs, and spices. For a bit of extra flavor, as well as a dose of healthy fat, this tapenade is amazingly versatile—try it as a spread for Rosemary Crackers (page 168) or Crunchy Multi-Seed Crackers (page 169), add it to lettuce wraps filled with deli meat, or simply use as a dip for cucumber rounds or veggie sticks.*

½ cup kalamata olives, pitted, rinsed, and minced

2 tablespoons capers, rinsed, drained, and minced

1 tablespoon finely diced red onion

1 tablespoon finely diced seeded red bell pepper

1 garlic clove, minced

1 tablespoon fresh lemon zest, minced

1 tablespoon finely chopped fresh oregano

¼ teaspoon crushed red pepper flakes

2 teaspoons olive oil

1. Place all the ingredients in a small bowl, and stir to combine. Serve immediately, or cover and refrigerate for up to 5 days.

Salmon Salad–Stuffed Cucumber Canapés

MAKES ABOUT 16 CANAPÉS   PREP TIME: 15 MINUTES   COOK TIME: NONE

● ● ●   *Spicy salmon salad, made with Homemade Mayonnaise stuffed into crisp cucumber rounds, makes for a satisfying and elegant appetizer full of protein and healthy fats. The salmon salad will keep for a couple of days in the refrigerator, so you can make the salad ahead of time and spoon it onto cucumber rounds for a quick afternoon nosh.*

¼ cup Homemade Mayonnaise (page 364)
¼ teaspoon smoked paprika
¼ teaspoon hot pepper sauce
½ teaspoon salt
¼ teaspoon freshly ground black pepper
½ pound cooked salmon, flaked
1 large English cucumber, peeled and cut crosswise into
    ¾-inch-thick slices
Parsley sprigs, for garnish (optional)

1. In a medium bowl, add the Homemade Mayonnaise, smoked paprika, and hot pepper sauce, and stir to combine. Add the salt and pepper, and stir to mix well. Add the salmon and mix gently.

2. Using a teaspoon or melon baller, scoop out the centers of the cucumber slices, leaving a layer on the bottom to form a cup. Arrange the cucumber cups on a serving platter, and spoon the salmon salad evenly into the cups. Top each with a sprig of parsley (if using), and serve immediately.

Smoky Prosciutto-Wrapped Squash Skewers

MAKES ABOUT 24 SKEWERS   PREP TIME: 10 MINUTES   COOK TIME: 20 MINUTES

● ● ●   *You often see recipes similar to this using shrimp. Here butternut squash is a delicious—and more affordable—stand-in. Prosciutto is a bit of a splurge, but you don't need a lot of it. You will need about 35 to 40 wooden skewers that have been soaked in water for about 30 minutes.*

1 tablespoon olive oil

1 garlic clove, minced

1 teaspoon ground chipotle pepper

1 teaspoon freshly ground black pepper

¼ teaspoon salt

½ small butternut squash, peeled, seeded, and cut like French fries

8 ounces very thinly sliced prosciutto, cut into strips

1. Preheat the oven to 350°F. Line a backing sheet with parchment paper.

2. In a large bowl, stir together the olive oil, garlic, chipotle pepper, black pepper, and salt. Add the squash sticks and toss to coat well.

3. Wrap a squash stick with a strip of prosciutto and lay it on the prepared baking sheet. Repeat with the remaining squash and prosciutto.

4. Bake for about 20 minutes, turning once halfway through, until the prosciutto is crisp and the squash is tender. Allow to cool 5 minutes, then serve.

Zucchini Pesto Rolls

SERVES 4   PREP TIME: 5 MINUTES   COOK TIME: NONE

These simple rolls possess all the flavors of a great pasta dish, without any pesky, grain-laden pasta. Serve them up as a pretty party appetizer—or just a great afternoon snack.

1 medium zucchini, sliced thin lengthwise

¼ cup Fresh Basil Pesto (page 365)

1 cup tomato sauce

½ cup toasted pine nuts

¼ cup Cashew Cheese (page 373)

1. Place a strip of zucchini on the work surface. Spread a tablespoon of Fresh Basil Pesto over the zucchini, followed by a layer of tomato sauce, and then top with pine nuts and a drizzle of Cashew Cheese.

2. Starting at one end, roll up the zucchini strip, and secure with a toothpick if needed. Repeat with the remaining zucchini strips and filling.

3. Serve immediately.

Chipotle Guacamole

SERVES 4 PREP TIME: 5 MINUTES COOK TIME: NONE

● ● ●   *Avocados are loaded with healthy fats and satisfying flavor. This quick guacamole is spiced with smoky chipotle pepper, giving it a bit of a kick. Serve it with fresh veggie sticks, cucumber rounds, or Crunchy Multi-Seed Crackers (page 169) for dipping.*

1 ripe avocado

1 medium tomato, seeded and diced

1½ tablespoons finely diced red onion

1 tablespoon freshly squeezed lime juice

1 tablespoon minced fresh cilantro

⅛ to ¼ teaspoon ground chipotle pepper

1. Halve the avocado, remove the pit, and use a large spoon to scoop the flesh out into a medium bowl. Mash the avocado with a fork, leaving it a bit lumpy.

2. Add the tomato, onion, lime juice, cilantro, and chipotle pepper, and stir to mix well. Serve immediately.

TIP   Be sure to use Haas avocadoes (the kind with bumpy black skin), because they have the right creamy texture for guacamole. Choose fruit that is firm but has a bit of give when you gently press the stem end with your thumb.

Roasted Red Pepper Garlic Hummus

SERVES 8 TO I2 (MAKES ABOUT 4 CUPS)   PREP TIME: 5 MINUTES   COOK TIME: NONE

Using canned chickpeas, roasted red peppers, and tahini (sesame paste) makes quick work of this flavorful hummus. This fresh, garlicky hummus will disappear before your eyes. Serve it with fresh vegetable sticks, Rosemary Crackers (page 168), or Crunchy Multi-Seed Crackers (see page 169) for dipping.

2 (15-ounce) cans chickpeas, drained and rinsed
¼ cup roasted red bell pepper, seeded and chopped
2 tablespoons freshly squeezed lemon juice
2 tablespoons tahini
3 garlic cloves, minced
¼ cup water
Salt

1. Put the chickpeas, bell pepper, lemon juice, tahini, and garlic in a food processor or blender. Blend until smooth.

2. Add the water and mix well. Add more water, if needed, to thin the mixture.

3. Season with salt and chill until ready to serve.

4. This hummus can be stored in the refrigerator in a sealed container for 3 to 4 days.

Roasted Cauliflower Hummus

SERVES 4   PREP TIME: 10 MINUTES   COOK TIME: 20 MINUTES

● ● ●   *Traditional hummus made with chickpeas is relatively high in carbohydrates, but this cauliflower version—which acquires similar flavors from the tahini (sesame paste) and lemon juice—is just as delicious and satisfying. The cauliflower develops a deep, complex sweetness through roasting and blends into a velvety smooth purée. Try it as a dip for veggie sticks, Rosemary Crackers (page 168), or Crunchy Multi-Seed Crackers (page 169), or use as a lettuce wrap filling.*

1 head cauliflower, cut into florets

2 tablespoons olive oil, plus 2 tablespoons, plus more
    for garnish

2 teaspoons ground cumin

1 teaspoon paprika, plus more for garnish

½ teaspoon salt

½ cup tahini

2 tablespoons freshly squeezed lemon juice

4 garlic cloves, minced

1. Preheat the oven to 500°F. Line a large baking sheet with parchment paper.

2. Toss the cauliflower, 2 tablespoons of the olive oil, cumin, paprika, and salt together in a large bowl. Spread the mixture out in a single layer on the prepared baking sheet and roast in the oven for about 20 minutes, until the cauliflower is soft and beginning to brown.

3. Transfer the cauliflower to a food processor or blender, add the remaining 2 tablespoons of olive oil, tahini, lemon juice, and garlic, and process into a smooth purée.

4. Serve the hummus topped with a drizzle of olive oil and a sprinkling of paprika.

Dijon Deviled Eggs

SERVES 6   PREP TIME: 10 MINUTES   COOK TIME: 15 MINUTES

Deviled eggs are a classic party dish, and this old-school version, spiked with Dijon mustard, won't disappoint. You can add any number of additional ingredients for variety—minced anchovies, minced chiles, chopped capers, minced chives, minced kalamata olives, or hot sauce.

6 hard-boiled eggs, cooled

1½ tablespoons Homemade Mayonnaise (page 364)

1 tablespoon Dijon mustard

3 tablespoons finely diced celery

1 tablespoon minced onion

3 tablespoons minced fresh flat-leaf parsley

¼ to ½ teaspoon salt

¼ teaspoon freshly ground black pepper

1. Carefully peel the hard-boiled eggs, and halve them lengthwise.

2. Scoop the yolks into a small bowl. Arrange the egg whites on a serving dish.

3. Mash the egg yolks with a fork, and stir in the Homemade Mayonnaise, Dijon mustard, celery, onion, and parsley. Add the salt and pepper, and stir to combine.

4. Spoon or pipe the egg-yolk filling into the egg whites.

5. Cover and chill up to 6 hours until ready to serve.

TIP   Use a pastry bag to pipe the filling into the egg whites for a simple but professional looking presentation. If you don't have a reusable pastry bag, inexpensive disposable pastry bags are available at most supermarkets. You can also make your own by snipping the corner off of a heavy-duty zip-top bag.

Rosemary Crackers

MAKES ABOUT 24 CRACKERS   PREP TIME: 10 MINUTES   COOK TIME: 20 MINUTES

These crisp, grain-free crackers are a tasty accompaniment to Roasted Cauliflower Hummus (page 165) or Cashew Cheese (page 373). You can create variety in flavor by using different herbs or spices, such as thyme, oregano, crushed red pepper, cracked pepper, or garlic powder.

2 cups almond meal

½ teaspoon salt

2 tablespoons minced fresh rosemary leaves

1 egg white

2 tablespoons water

1 tablespoon olive oil

¼ teaspoon coconut oil, melted

1. Preheat the oven to 350°F.

2. In a medium bowl, stir together the almond meal, salt, and rosemary.

3. In a separate medium bowl, whisk together the egg white, water, olive oil, and coconut oil.

4. Add the egg mixture to the almond meal mixture, and stir to combine well. You should now have a stiff dough.

5. Place a piece of parchment paper on your work surface, and transfer the dough to it. Top with a second piece of parchment, and roll the dough out to about ⅛-inch thick. Peel off the top piece of parchment paper, and transfer the bottom sheet, with the rolled dough on it, to a baking sheet. Trim the edges square using a pizza or pastry cutter, then cut the sheet of dough into 2-by-2-inch squares.

6. Bake the crackers for about 10 minutes. Turn off the oven but leave the crackers for another 10 minutes, during which time they will turn crisp and golden brown. Transfer the crackers to a wire rack to cool. Serve at room temperature.

Crunchy Multi-Seed Crackers

SERVES 4 TO 6   PREP TIME: 5 MINUTES   COOK TIME: 50 MINUTES

● ● ●   *These crunchy crackers contain no grains or dairy. What they do contain is a whole lot of healthy fats, omega-3 fatty acids, protein, fiber, and minerals, not to mention delicious nutty flavor. Be sure to find pepitas, the soft interior pumpkin seeds inside the woody shells. They make an excellent snack on their own, and are also perfect for dipping in Roasted Red Pepper Garlic Hummus (page 164), Roasted Cauliflower Hummus (page 165), or Olive Tapenade (page 158).*

¾ cup chia seeds

½ cup pumpkin seeds (pepitas)

½ cup sunflower seeds

¼ cup sesame seeds

1 cup water

¼ teaspoon salt

1. In a medium bowl, stir together the chia seeds, pumpkin seeds, sunflower seeds, sesame seeds, water, and salt. Let the mixture sit for about 30 minutes, during which time the chia seeds will absorb the water and form a thick gel that will hold the dough together.

2. Meanwhile, preheat the oven to 325°F. Line a baking sheet with parchment paper.

3. Spread the dough on the prepared baking sheet about ¼-inch thick.

4. Bake for 30 minutes. Remove from the oven and use a pizza wheel or pastry cutter to slice the crackers into 2-inch squares.

5. Flip the cracker squares over carefully, and bake for 20 to 25 minutes.

6. Cool the crackers completely before serving. Store in an airtight container at room temperature for up to 5 days.

Crispy Baked Onion Rings

SERVES 6   PREP TIME: 5 MINUTES   COOK TIME: 25 MINUTES

Usually dipped in a flour-based batter, traditional onion rings are a no-no on the sugar detox diet. This crispy, crunchy version replaces the customary flour in batter with almond meal, which not only makes them permissible on this program, but adds a boost of protein and healthy fats as well. This nutritious version of the classic burger-joint side dish is seriously tasty. Serve them with a bowl of Sugar-Free Ketchup (page 366), if desired.

Coconut oil for the pan

1 cup coconut milk

1 egg

1 cup almond meal

½ teaspoon salt, plus more for serving

¼ teaspoon garlic powder

1 large yellow onion, cut into ½-inch-thick slices
and separated into rings

1. Preheat the oven to 450°F. Lightly coat a large baking sheet with coconut oil.

2. In a shallow bowl, whisk together the coconut milk and egg. In a separate shallow bowl, stir together the almond meal, salt, and garlic powder.

3. Dip the onion rings, one at a time, first into the coconut milk–egg mixture and then into the almond meal mixture, and arrange them on the prepared baking sheet in a single layer.

4. Bake for 15 minutes. Remove the pan from the oven, and flip over each onion ring. Return to the oven and cook for about 10 minutes, until golden brown and crispy.

5. Serve immediately, seasoned with additional salt, if desired.

Crispy Pepperoni Pizza Bites

SERVES 8 (MAKES ABOUT 24 MINI PIZZAS)
PREP TIME: 10 MINUTES   COOK TIME: 20 MINUTES

Crispy rounds of spicy pepperoni stand in for traditional pizza crust here. Topped with sun-dried tomato pesto, mushrooms, and fresh basil, these little pizza bites are delicious and satisfying. If you prefer a milder version, substitute salami for the pepperoni. You might also top the bites with a drizzle of Cashew Cheese (page 373), if desired.

6 ounces large sliced pepperoni

½ cup sun-dried tomato pesto or oil-packed sun-dried tomatoes, drained and minced

½ cup finely diced mushrooms

½ cup chopped fresh basil

1. Preheat the oven to 400°F. Line a baking sheet with parchment paper.

2. Arrange the pepperoni slices in a single layer on the prepared baking sheet, and bake for about 8 minutes, until crispy, turning the slices over after about 4 minutes.

3. Remove the baking sheet from the oven, and top each pepperoni slice with about 1 teaspoon of the sun-dried tomato pesto. Sprinkle about 1 teaspoon of the mushrooms. Return the baking sheet to the oven and bake for 5 to 10 minutes, until the pesto is hot and bubbly and the mushrooms are cooked.

4. Serve immediately, garnished with the basil.

Creamy Avocado Spinach Dip

MAKES ABOUT 2 CUPS PREP TIME: 5 MINUTES COOK TIME: NONE

● ● ● *In this dish, avocado stands in for the usual sour cream, replacing its texture and adding healthy fats and delicious flavor. Served with veggie sticks, Rosemary Crackers (page 168), or Crunchy Multi-Seed Crackers (page 169), this dip makes a perfect game day appetizer or anytime snack.*

5 cups raw spinach
1 large avocado
½ onion
1 clove garlic
½ teaspoon salt
Juice of 1 freshly squeezed lemon

Place all the ingredients in a food processor or blender, and process until smooth. Serve immediately.

TEN

SOUPS, SALADS, AND SIDES

Butternut Squash and Chipotle Soup

SERVES 6   PREP TIME: 10 MINUTES   COOK TIME: 45 MINUTES

● ● ●   *An excellent source of beta-carotene, naturally sweet butternut squash pairs beautifully with the smoky heat of ground chipotle chile. If you are on the yellow or green plan, try garnishing with a dollop of plain yogurt, which adds a cooling element and creamy texture.*

2 tablespoons olive oil

1 small onion, chopped

2 garlic cloves, minced

1 teaspoon ground cumin

1 teaspoon salt

¼ teaspoon freshly ground black pepper

¼ to ½ teaspoon ground chipotle pepper

⅛ teaspoon ground cloves

1½ pounds peeled and cubed butternut squash (about 1 medium squash)

1 medium carrot, diced

1 stalk celery, diced

6 cups vegetable broth

2 tablespoons snipped fresh chives, for garnish

1. Heat the olive oil in a large stockpot over medium-high heat. Add the onion and garlic, and cook, stirring frequently, for about 5 minutes, until softened. Stir in the cumin, salt, black pepper, chipotle pepper, and cloves, and cook, still stirring, for 1 minute. Add the squash, carrot, celery, and vegetable broth, and bring to a boil. Reduce the heat to medium-low and simmer for 35 to 40 minutes, until the squash is tender.

2. Using an immersion blender or a blender (in batches), purée the soup.

3. Reheat the soup over medium heat until warmed through. Serve hot, garnished with chives.

TIP   This soup keeps well either in the refrigerator or freezer. Store covered in the refrigerator for up to 5 days, or freeze in individual-size servings for up to 3 months.

Vegetable Minestrone with White Beans

SERVES 4   PREP TIME: 10 MINUTES   COOK TIME: 50 MINUTES

This classic Italian soup traditionally contains pasta, but here it features vegetables that deliver vitamins, minerals, and fiber, along with cannellini beans, adding plenty of protein without too much carbohydrate. A finishing touch of optional grated Parmesan cheese rounds out the flavor. This soup keeps well, so make a big pot and enjoy it all week.

3 ounces bacon
1 small onion, finely diced
1 stalk celery, diced
1 medium carrot, diced
Olive oil, if needed
3 garlic cloves, minced
1 teaspoon salt
½ teaspoon freshly ground black pepper
4 cups baby spinach or other dark leafy greens
2 medium zucchini, diced
1 (15-ounce) can diced tomatoes with the juice
1 cup fresh flat-leaf parsley, chopped
6 cups chicken broth
1 (15-ounce) can cannellini beans, drained and rinsed
2 ounces grated Parmesan cheese

1. Cook the bacon in a large stockpot over medium-high heat for about 4 minutes per side, until crisp. Drain on paper towels and crumble.

2. Add the onion, celery, and carrot to the bacon fat in the stockpot (if it's not enough, you can add a bit of olive oil) and cook, stirring frequently, for about 5 minutes, until the vegetables begin to soften. Stir in the garlic, salt, and pepper, and cook for 1 to 2 minutes.

3. Add the spinach, zucchini, tomatoes, parsley, and chicken broth and bring to a boil. Reduce the heat to medium-low and simmer for about 20 minutes.

4. While the soup is simmering, place about one-half of the beans in a food processor or blender and process until smooth. Add the puréed beans and the remaining whole beans to the soup, along with the crumbled bacon, and continue to simmer for about 15 minutes.

5. Serve hot, sprinkled with the Parmesan cheese. Store leftovers in the refrigerator for up to 1 week or in the freezer for up to 3 months.

> TIP   To make this soup vegetarian, simply eliminate the bacon, cook the veggies in 2 tablespoons olive oil, and substitute vegetable broth for the chicken broth.

Leek, Fennel, and Turnip Soup

SERVES 6   PREP TIME: 5 MINUTES   COOK TIME: 25 MINUTES

Turnips thicken this soup instead of the usual potatoes and cream. As a result, the soup is lighter but no less satisfying. Meanwhile, the fennel gives it a rich and distinctive flavor. This simple soup can be made either with chicken broth, or, if you prefer a meatless version, with vegetable broth.

- 2 tablespoons olive oil
- 3 large leeks, white and light green parts, cleaned and thinly sliced
- 4 large stalks celery, thinly sliced
- 3 large white onions, peeled and halved
- 1 large fennel bulb, trimmed and thinly sliced
- 2 large turnips, peeled and cut into ½-inch cubes
- 1 tablespoon salt, plus more if needed
- 1½ teaspoons freshly ground black pepper, plus more if needed
- 8 cups chicken broth or vegetable broth

1. Heat the olive oil in a large stockpot over medium-high heat. Add the leeks, celery, onions, fennel, turnips, salt, and pepper, and cook, stirring frequently, for about 5 minutes, until the vegetables begin to soften.

2. Add the chicken broth and bring to a boil. Reduce the heat to medium-low, and simmer for about 20 minutes, until the vegetables are tender and the turnips have begun to thicken the soup.

3. Purée the soup using an immersion blender or a countertop blender (in batches). Reheat the soup over medium heat until warmed through. Taste and adjust the seasoning as needed. Serve hot.

Cream of Artichoke and Spinach Soup

SERVES 4   PREP TIME: 5 MINUTES   COOK TIME: 20 MINUTES

● ● ● *Coconut cream stands in for the dairy you'd normally use to make this soup creamy. Asian markets often sell cans of coconut cream, but if you can't find it, simply chill a regular can of full-fat coconut milk, open it, and scoop off the thick cream that has risen to the top (you can save the thinner portion for another use). You'll get about 1 cup of cream from a 13½-ounce can of coconut milk.*

2 tablespoons olive oil

1 medium onion, chopped

2 garlic cloves, minced

10 ounces fresh spinach

1 (14-ounce) can artichoke hearts, drained

3 cups chicken broth or vegetable broth

1 teaspoon salt

½ teaspoon freshly ground black pepper

1 cup coconut cream

1. Heat the olive oil in a large stockpot over medium-high heat. Add the onion and cook, stirring frequently, for about 5 minutes, until softened. Add the garlic and continue to cook, stirring, for 1 minute more. Stir in the spinach and artichoke hearts, and cook until the spinach wilts, about 2 minutes.

2. Add the chicken broth, salt, and pepper, and bring to a boil. Reduce the heat to medium-low and simmer for 10 minutes.

3. Stir the coconut cream into the soup, and then purée with an immersion blender, or in a blender (in batches).

4. Reheat the soup over medium heat until warmed through. Serve hot.

Tortilla-Less Chicken Soup

SERVES 8   PREP TIME: 10 MINUTES   COOK TIME: 20 MINUTES

● ● ●   *This simple soup is based on the traditional chicken tortilla soup thickened with corn tortillas. This version maintains the spicy Mexican flavor of the classic version—including garlic, chiles, chili powder, oregano, cilantro, and lime—but without the use of tortillas or other grains.*

2 tablespoons olive oil

1 large onion, diced

4 garlic cloves, minced

2 jalapeño chiles, seeded and diced

2 poblano chilies, seeded and diced

1 teaspoon ground cumin

1 teaspoon chili powder

1 teaspoon dried oregano

1 teaspoon salt

½ teaspoon freshly ground black pepper

¼ teaspoon cayenne pepper

8 cups chicken broth

1 (28-ounce) can diced tomatoes, drained

2 pounds cooked, shredded chicken breast

1 cup chopped fresh cilantro, plus more for garnish

Juice of 2 freshly squeezed limes

1 medium avocado, diced

1. Heat the olive oil in a large stockpot over medium-high heat. Add the onion and cook, stirring frequently, for about 5 minutes, until the onions are soft. Add the garlic, jalapeño chiles, and poblano chiles, and cook, stirring frequently, for about 2 minutes. Stir in the cumin, chili powder, oregano, salt, black pepper, and cayenne pepper. Add the chicken broth and tomatoes and bring to a boil. ▶

2. Reduce the heat to medium, add the chicken, and cook about 10 minutes, until heated through. Just before serving, stir in the cilantro and lime juice.

3. Serve hot, topped with avocado and garnished with cilantro.

Tom Ka Gai
(Thai Chicken–
Coconut Milk Soup)

SERVES 6   PREP TIME: 10 MINUTES   COOK TIME: 20 MINUTES

● ● ● *A Thai restaurant favorite, this hearty soup is enriched with coconut milk and nutirious chunks of chicken. Lime juice, fish sauce, and chiles enrich the dish with complex flavor, while mushrooms and broccoli make it a complete meal in a bowl.*

1 tablespoon coconut oil

3 shallots, chopped

2 teaspoons Thai red curry paste

2 (13½-ounce) cans coconut milk

4 cups chicken broth

8 sprigs cilantro, chopped, plus ½ cup minced cilantro, for garnish

½ pound button or cremini mushrooms

1 head broccoli

2 skinless, boneless chicken breasts halved lengthwise and sliced against the grain into ⅛-inch-thick strips

3 tablespoons freshly squeezed lime juice

1 tablespoon fish sauce

1. Heat the coconut oil in a large stockpot over medium-high heat. Add the shallots and cook, stirring frequently, for about 5 minutes, until softened. Stir in the curry paste and cook, stirring, for 1 minute more. Add the coconut milk, chicken broth, and cilantro, and bring to a boil. Reduce the heat to medium-low and simmer for about 5 minutes. ▶

2. Strain the broth through a fine mesh sieve, discard the solids, and return the broth to the stockpot over medium-high heat. Add the mushrooms and broccoli, and cook for about 3 minutes, until softened. Reduce the heat to medium, add the chicken, and cook until fully opaque, about 3 minutes.

3. Just before serving, add the lime juice and fish sauce and stir to combine. Serve hot, garnished with minced cilantro.

Italian Sausage Soup with Greens

SERVES 6 PREP TIME: 5 MINUTES COOK TIME: 25 MINUTES

Turnips and almond milk stand in for the potatoes and cream that would normally be used to thicken this soup—and this version is every bit as mouthwatering as the original. You can use spicy or mild sausage, depending on your taste.

1 pound Italian sausage

1 medium onion, diced

3 garlic cloves, diced

1 teaspoon crushed red pepper flakes (optional)

8 cups chicken broth

4 medium turnips, peeled and diced

4 cups chopped fresh kale

1 cup unsweetened almond milk

1 teaspoon salt

½ teaspoon freshly ground black pepper

1. Heat a large stockpot over medium-high heat. Add the sausage to the pan and cook, stirring and breaking up the meat with a spatula, for about 5 minutes, until thoroughly browned.

2. Add the onion and garlic and cook, stirring frequently, for about 5 minutes, until the onion is softened. Stir in the red pepper flakes.

3. Add the chicken broth and turnips, and bring to a boil. Reduce the heat to low and simmer for about 10 minutes. Stir in the kale and almond milk, and continue to simmer about 5 minutes, until the turnips and kale are tender and the soup is heated through.

4. Add the salt and pepper and stir to combine. Serve hot.

Avocado, Tomato, and Basil Salad

SERVES 4   PREP TIME: 5 MINUTES   COOK TIME: NONE

The Italian classic Caprese salad is made with tomatoes, fresh mozzarella cheese, and fresh basil. In this version, rich, creamy avocado stands in for the mozzarella. Paired with juicy heirloom tomatoes and fresh basil, and dressed with lemon juice and olive oil, this delectable, wholesome salad works equally well as a starter or side.

3 medium avocados, sliced

4 medium heirloom tomatoes, diced

1 large bunch fresh basil leaves

Juice of 1 freshly squeezed lemon

½ teaspoon salt

¼ teaspoon freshly ground black pepper

Olive oil

2 tablespoons shredded Parmesan cheese

2 tablespoons toasted pine nuts

1. In a medium bowl, gently toss the avocados, tomatoes, and basil with the lemon juice.

2. Add the salt and pepper and drizzle with the oil.

3. Sprinkle the Parmesan and pine nuts over the top and serve immediately.

Broccoli Salad with Warm Bacon Vinaigrette

SERVES 4   PREP TIME: 10 MINUTES   COOK TIME: 10 MINUTES

Studded with crisp, tart apples and crumbles of smoky bacon, this broccoli salad is sure to be a hit. In fact, enhanced with a warm vinaigrette and a sprinkling of chopped walnuts, it might just become the favorite salad on your household menu.

2 small heads of broccoli, cut into small florets (4 to 5 cups)

8 slices bacon

1 small shallot, finely diced

1 teaspoon Dijon mustard

1 tablespoon apple cider vinegar

½ teaspoon salt

½ teaspoon freshly ground black pepper

½ small red onion, thinly sliced

2 small, crisp green apples, cored and thinly sliced

2 tablespoons chopped walnuts

1. Bring a large pot of salted water to a boil. Add the broccoli and parboil for about 60 seconds, just long enough to remove the rawness. Drain and transfer to a bowl of ice water to stop the cooking. Drain again and place in a large salad bowl.

2. Heat a large skillet over medium-high heat. Add the bacon and cook for 6 to 8 minutes, turning once, until crisp. Transfer the bacon to a paper towel–lined plate to drain. Reserve about 3 tablespoons of the bacon fat in the skillet.

3. Add the shallot to the hot bacon fat in the skillet, reduce the heat to medium, and cook for about 3 minutes, until it begins to soften. Remove from the heat, and immediately stir in the mustard, vinegar, salt, and pepper, and whisk to combine.

4. Add the onion and apples to the broccoli, and toss to combine. Pour the warm dressing over the broccoli, and toss well. Add the walnuts and toss again to combine. Serve immediately, while still warm.

Grilled Romaine and Bacon Salad

SERVES 4   PREP TIME: 5 MINUTES   COOK TIME: I5 MINUTES

The sugar detox diet—or any low-carb eating plan—can cause salad fatigue. Grilling the lettuce offers an interesting twist. And, of course, topping the slightly smoky grilled lettuce with garlicky tomatoes and crisp bacon only enhances the salad further.

2 teaspoons olive oil

8 strips bacon

2 small heads Romaine lettuce, halved lengthwise

2 large tomatoes, diced

2 garlic cloves, minced

2 tablespoons chopped fresh flat-leaf parsley, for garnish

½ lemon, squeezed for garnish

1. Heat an outdoor grill or grill pan to high heat, and brush the grill with the olive oil.

2. Heat a medium skillet over medium-high heat, and cook the bacon for 6 to 8 minutes, until crispy, turning once. Transfer to paper towels to drain and then crumble.

3. Place the lettuce, cut-side down, on the preheated grill. Place a heavy plate or pan lid on top to ensure that the lettuce makes full contact with the grill. Cook for 2 to 3 minutes per side, until charred.

4. Add the tomatoes to the bacon grease in the pan, and cook for about 4 minutes, until they begin to break down. Add the garlic and cook for 2 to 3 minutes, stirring frequently.

5. To serve, place a grilled lettuce wedge on each of 4 serving plates. Top each evenly with the tomato mixture, and sprinkle the bacon over the top.

6. Serve immediately, garnished with parsley and a squeeze of lemon juice.

Lemony Cauliflower "Rice" Salad with Apples and Spinach

SERVES 4   PREP TIME: I5 MINUTES   COOK TIME: NONE

● ● ●   *This quick salad is studded with tart apple, crunchy hazelnuts, and crisp, fresh spinach leaves, and tossed with a bright dressing of fresh herbs and lemon. Serve it anytime you'd serve a traditional rice salad.*

⅓ cup fresh basil

⅓ cup fresh cilantro

⅓ cup fresh parsley

3 tablespoons olive oil

Juice of 1 lemon

½ teaspoon salt

1 garlic clove, minced

2 cups Cauliflower "Rice" (page 372)

1 large green apple, cored and cut into matchsticks

½ cup hazelnuts, lightly toasted

2 cups baby spinach leaves, cut into ribbons

Freshly ground black pepper, for garnish

1. To make the vinaigrette, in a food processor or blender, add the basil, cilantro, parsley, olive oil, lemon juice, salt, and garlic, and process until well combined.

2. In a large bowl, add the Cauliflower "Rice," apple, hazelnuts, and spinach, and toss to combine. Drizzle the vinaigrette over the top, and toss again to coat. Serve immediately, garnished with pepper.

Rainbow Slaw with Spiced Citrus Vinaigrette

SERVES 6   PREP TIME: 10 MINUTES   COOK TIME: NONE

●●● *This bright and crunchy slaw is a welcome change from the more common mayonnaise-heavy version. Root veggies are shredded and tossed with a bright dressing of sherry vinegar, orange juice, and toasted cumin seeds. This salad can certainly be eaten straightaway, but its flavor actually improves as it sits, so feel free to make it 30 minutes or more in advance.*

Zest and juice of 2 lemons

1 teaspoon toasted whole cumin seeds

3 tablespoons sherry vinegar

1 tablespoon olive oil

¾ teaspoon salt

½ teaspoon freshly ground black pepper

½ small head red cabbage, shredded

2 medium carrots, peeled and shredded

2 medium red, orange, or golden beets, peeled and shredded

1 small celery root, peeled and shredded

1. Whisk together the lemon zest, lemon juice, cumin seeds, vinegar, olive oil, salt, and pepper in a large salad bowl.

2. Add the cabbage, carrots, beets, and celery root, and toss to coat well.

3. Serve immediately or refrigerate, covered, for up to 3 days.

Oven-Roasted Radishes

SERVES 4   PREP TIME: 5 MINUTES   COOK TIME: 25 MINUTES

The radish is one of those vegetables—like lettuce or avocados—that few people ever think to cook. Slow-roasting radishes mellows their flavor to a subtle sweetness. Serve this dish alongside any roasted, seared, or grilled meat or fish—it's especially nice with roast duck.

2 bunches radishes, trimmed and halved lengthwise

2½ tablespoons olive oil

2 tablespoons freshly squeezed lemon juice

½ teaspoon salt

¼ teaspoon freshly ground black pepper

1 teaspoon fresh lemon zest

1. Preheat the oven to 375°F. Line a large baking sheet with parchment paper.

2. In a large bowl, add the radishes, olive oil, lemon juice, salt, and pepper, and toss to coat.

3. Transfer the mixture to the prepared baking sheet, and roast for 20 to 25 minutes, until the radishes are fork tender and beginning to turn brown and crisp around the edges.

4. Transfer to a serving bowl and sprinkle with lemon zest. Serve warm.

Asparagus and Avocado Salad

SERVES 4   PREP TIME: I0 MINUTES   COOK TIME: 7 MINUTES

Made with tender asparagus and creamy avocado, this salad is surprisingly hearty. Its green hues of are punctuated by bright red cherry tomatoes, making this salad both attractive and delicious.

- 1 pound asparagus spears, woody ends snapped off and discarded, spears cut into 2-inch lengths
- 1 cup halved cherry tomatoes
- 1 avocado, diced
- ¼ cup packed basil leaves
- ¼ cup olive oil
- 2 teaspoons freshly squeezed lemon juice
- 1 teaspoon balsamic vinegar
- 1 teaspoon Dijon mustard
- ½ teaspoon salt
- ¼ teaspoon freshly ground black pepper

1. Place the asparagus in a steamer basket inside a large lidded saucepan, and add about 2 inches of water. Bring the water to a boil over medium-high heat, cover, and steam the asparagus for about 5 minutes, until just fork-tender. Drain and let cool for a few minutes.

2. In a large serving bowl, add the asparagus, tomatoes, avocado, and basil, and toss to mix. ▶

3. In a small bowl, whisk together the olive oil, lemon juice, vinegar, and mustard. Pour the dressing over the salad, and toss to coat.

4. Season with salt and pepper and toss again. Serve warm.

TIP   To prepare asparagus for cooking, snap off the woody, fibrous ends by bending the asparagus stalk near the bottom. The spear will snap and break where the woody part begins.

Curry-Roasted Cauliflower

SERVES 4   PREP TIME: 5 MINUTES   COOK TIME 40 MINUTES

Roasted cauliflower takes on a deep, complex sweetness, further enhanced here by curry powder and garam masala. This simple dish is a perfect match for grilled steak but also pairs well with chicken, fish, or shellfish.

1 medium head cauliflower, cut into small florets

1 tablespoon coconut oil

2 teaspoons curry powder

1 teaspoon garam masala

½ teaspoon paprika

½ teaspoon salt

¼ teaspoon freshly ground black pepper

1 cup chicken broth

1. Preheat the oven to 375°F.

2. Place the cauliflower in a large baking dish and toss with the coconut oil, curry powder, garam masala, paprika, salt, and pepper. Pour the chicken broth over the cauliflower mixture.

3. Bake for 35 to 40 minutes, tossing about every 10 minutes, until the cauliflower is tender and beginning to crisp around the edges. Serve immediately.

TIP   Garam masala is a spice mixture commonly found in Northern Indian cooking. To make your own, combine 1 tablespoon ground cumin, 1½ teaspoons each ground coriander, ground cardamom, and ground pepper, 1 teaspoon ground cinnamon, and ½ teaspoon each ground cloves and ground nutmeg.

Zucchini and Pistachio Salad

SERVES 4 PREP TIME: 15 MINUTES COOK TIME: NONE

● ● ●   *Anyone with a vegetable garden is familiar with the late summer zucchini glut. This recipe is a great way to use up some of that bountiful produce. If you don't grow your own, visit your local farmers' market any time from June through August, and you'll find plenty of summer squash varieties from which to choose.*

3 medium zucchini, thinly sliced

2 tablespoons chopped fresh basil

2 tablespoons olive oil

1 tablespoon freshly squeezed lemon juice

1 teaspoon balsamic vinegar

Pinch of salt

Pinch of freshly ground black pepper

2 tablespoons chopped pistachios

1. In a medium bowl, toss together the zucchini and basil.

2. In a small bowl, whisk together the olive oil, lemon juice, vinegar, salt, and pepper. Pour the dressing over the vegetables and toss to coat.

3. Garnish with the pistachios, and serve at room temperature or slightly chilled.

TIP   For this salad, use any type of soft-skinned summer squash, such as regular zucchini, yellow zucchini, crookneck, or pattypan squash.

Mashed Parsnips
with Garlic

SERVES 4   PREP TIME: 5 MINUTES   COOK TIME: 10 MINUTES

● ● ●   *This dish is like mashed potatoes without all the starch, so it's a perfect side to serve with pot roast, steak, or roast chicken or turkey.*

1 pound parsnips, peeled and diced
½ cup unsweetened almond milk
3 or 4 garlic cloves, roasted, or 1 clove fresh garlic, minced
2 tablespoons olive oil or coconut oil
Salt
Freshly ground black pepper

1. Put the parsnips in a large saucepan and cover with water by about 2 inches. Bring to a boil over high heat, reduce the heat to medium, and simmer for about 10 minutes, until the parsnips are tender. Drain.

2. Place the parsnips in a large bowl and mash with a potato masher or a hand-held immersion blender. Add the almond milk, garlic, and olive oil, and stir to combine. Season with salt and pepper, and serve immediately.

TIP   To roast garlic, preheat the oven to 400°F. Slice the top ½ inch off a whole head of garlic so the cloves are exposed. Place the head of garlic on a square of aluminum foil, and drizzle with about 1 tablespoon of olive oil. Wrap the foil loosely around the garlic, and bake for about 45 minutes, until the cloves are browned and very soft. Squeeze the cloves out of the skin to use. Store in the refrigerator for up to 1 week or in the freezer for up to 3 months.

Braised Brussels Sprouts with Shallots and Thyme

SERVES 4   PREP TIME: 5 MINUTES   COOK TIME: 20 MINUTES

When cooked properly, Brussels sprouts develop an almost nutty sweetness. This version pairs them with shallots and thyme, adding subtle layers of flavor to the mix. Serve alongside roasted or grilled meats, especially rich meats like steak, lamb, or duck.

1 tablespoon olive oil

1 pound Brussels sprouts, trimmed and halved

2 shallots, thinly sliced

1 cup chicken broth or vegetable broth

1½ teaspoons chopped fresh thyme

¼ teaspoon salt

¼ teaspoon freshly ground black pepper

1. Heat the olive oil in a large skillet over medium-high heat. Add the sprouts and shallots and cook, stirring frequently, for about 5 minutes, until the shallots are softened and the sprouts are beginning to brown.

2. Add the chicken broth, thyme, salt, and pepper. Reduce the heat to medium-low, cover, and cook for 10 to 15 minutes, until the sprouts are tender.

> TIP   If fresh thyme isn't available, you can substitute another fresh herb, such as sage or rosemary. Dried thyme will work in a pinch, but it won't provide the same fragrant quality as the fresh herb.

Zucchini Pancakes

SERVES 6
PREP TIME: IO MINUTES (PLUS IO MINUTES TO DRAIN ZUCCHINI)
COOK TIME: I5 MINUTES

These tasty fritters are easy to make and a great opportunity for using up excess zucchini you might have in your garden. You can grate the zucchini on a box grater, but by using a shredding blade in a food processor, you'll accomplish the task more quickly.

5 medium zucchini, shredded (about 4 cups)

2 teaspoons salt

¼ cup almond flour

1 egg, lightly beaten

1 teaspoon freshly ground black pepper

¼ teaspoon cayenne pepper

2 tablespoons coconut oil

1. Put the shredded zucchini in a colander and sprinkle with the salt. Toss to distribute the salt, and set the colander in the sink for about 10 minutes while the zucchini releases some of its moisture.

2. Wrap the zucchini in a clean, dry dish towel, and squeeze out as much moisture as possible.

3. In a large bowl, add the zucchini, almond flour, egg, black pepper, and cayenne pepper, and stir to mix well.

4. Heat some of the coconut oil in a large skillet over medium heat. Drop the zucchini mixture, ¼ cup at a time, into the pan, and flatten into a patty with the measuring cup or a spatula. Cook for about 3 minutes, until browned on the bottom, then flip over and cook for about 3 minutes, until browned on the other side. Repeat with the remaining zucchini mixture, adding more coconut oil to the pan as needed. Serve hot.

Spiced Broccoli with Toasted Coconut

SERVES 4   PREP TIME: 5 MINUTES   COOK TIME: I0 MINUTES

Broccoli is affordable, widely available year-round, and easy to cook. Are you looking for a tasty new way to prepare it? This version eliminates broccoli ennui with a kick of fresh ginger and fragrant curry powder and cumin. A sprinkling of toasted coconut adds even more flavor and a welcome textural contrast.

¼ cup unsweetened coconut flakes

1 tablespoon coconut oil

1 tablespoon minced fresh peeled ginger

½ small yellow onion, halved and thinly sliced

1 teaspoon cumin seeds

2 teaspoons curry powder

½ teaspoon salt

1 pound broccoli florets

2 tablespoons water

1. Heat a large skillet over medium heat and add the coconut flakes. Cook, stirring, for about 4 minutes, until the coconut begins to turn brown and toasty. Transfer the coconut to a small bowl.

2. Return the skillet to the stove top, add the coconut oil, and heat over medium-high heat. Add the ginger, onion, cumin seeds, curry powder, and salt, and cook, stirring frequently, for about 4 minutes, until the onion begin to soften and the spices are fragrant.

3. Stir in the broccoli florets and water. Cover, reduce the heat to low, and cook for about 4 minutes, until the broccoli is tender.

4. Transfer the broccoli to a serving platter, and sprinkle with the toasted coconut. Serve immediately.

Sautéed Chard with Shiitakes and Garlic

SERVES 4   PREP TIME: 5 MINUTES   COOK TIME: 12 MINUTES

● ● ●   *This simple dish is especially stunning if you use rainbow chard with stems ranging in color from yellow to bright orange to hot pink. Even if the rainbow variety is unavailable, this dish is still pretty using green or red chard and will be just as delicious.*

1 tablespoon olive oil

5 ounces shiitake mushrooms, sliced

1 pound Swiss chard, thick stems cut into ½-inch slices, leaves julienned

2 garlic cloves, minced

2 teaspoons chopped fresh thyme

¼ teaspoon salt

¼ teaspoon freshly ground black pepper

½ cup water

1. Heat the olive oil in a large skillet over medium-high heat. Add the mushrooms and chard stems and cook, stirring frequently, for about 3 minutes, until the mushrooms begin to soften and brown.

2. Stir in the garlic, thyme, salt, and pepper, and cook, stirring, for 30 seconds.

3. Add the chard leaves and cook, stirring frequently, for about 3 minutes, until the leaves are wilted.

4. Reduce the heat to medium-low, stir in the water, cover, and simmer for 3 minutes, until the chard is very tender. Serve immediately.

ELEVEN

FISH AND SEAFOOD

Grilled Prawns with Pesto

SERVES 4
PREP TIME: 5 MINUTES (PLUS 15 MINUTES TO MARINATE THE PRAWNS)
COOK TIME: 5 MINUTES

● ● ●   *If you've got a batch of Fresh Basil Pesto on hand, this recipe is a snap. But even if you're starting from scratch, you can easily have this dinner on the table in 30 minutes or less. You can use store-bought pesto instead, as long as it doesn't contain any added sugar (or cheese, if you're on the blue plan). Because this dish requires grilling, you'll need 6 to 8 wood skewers that have been soaked in water for about 30 minutes.*

1 pound peeled and deveined prawns
½ cup Fresh Basil Pesto (page 365)

1. In a medium bowl, toss together the prawns and Fresh Basil Pesto. Marinate in the refrigerator for about 15 minutes.

2. Heat a grill or grill pan to medium-high heat.

3. Thread the marinated prawns onto the skewers, 3 to 5 per skewer.

4. Grill the skewers for about 2 minutes per side, until the prawns are just cooked through. Serve immediately.

> **TIP**   Buying peeled and deveined prawns may cost a bit more than buying them in the shell and prepping them yourself, but if you're short on time, the minutes saved are well worth the money.

Shrimp Baked with Tomatoes and Garlic

SERVES 4   PREP TIME: 5 MINUTES   COOK TIME: 40 MINUTES

●●● *This easy-to-prepare casserole of plump shrimp baked in a rich tomato sauce spiked with garlic is simple and satisfying. A mixed green salad with vinaigrette is all you need to round out the meal. If you're on the yellow or green plan, try adding a sprinkling of Parmesan cheese to the top before baking.*

- 4 tablespoons olive oil
- ½ cup diced onion
- ½ cup diced green bell pepper
- 2 scallions, chopped
- 3 garlic cloves, minced
- ½ teaspoon salt
- ¼ teaspoon freshly ground black pepper
- 1 teaspoon paprika
- 1 teaspoon dried oregano
- 1 (15½-ounce) can diced tomatoes with the juice, or 2 large fresh tomatoes, seeded and diced
- 1 pound peeled and deveined medium shrimp
- 2 tablespoons chopped flat-leaf parsley, for garnish

1. Preheat the oven to 375°F.

2. Heat the olive oil in a large skillet over medium-high heat. Add the onion, bell pepper, scallions, and garlic, and cook, stirring frequently, for about 5 minutes, until the vegetables are soft. Stir in the salt, pepper, paprika, and oregano, then add the tomatoes. Cook, stirring occasionally, for about 15 minutes, until the liquid has been reduced by about half. Add the shrimp and cook for about 3 minutes, until it is just pink.

3. Transfer the mixture to a large baking dish, and bake for about 20 minutes. Serve immediately, garnished with the parsley.

Brazilian Garlic-Lime Shrimp

SERVES 4
PREP TIME: 5 MINUTES (PLUS 20 MINUTES TO MARINATE THE SHRIMP)
COOK TIME: 5 MINUTES

Sprightly garlic makes a powerful appearance in this quick and simple, but super flavorful shrimp dish that can be on the table in under half and hour. To save time, buy shrimp that's already been peeled and deveined. Serve with Cauliflower "Rice" (page 372) or sautéed Swiss chard for a complete meal.

- 2 pounds large peeled and deveined shrimp
- 2 tablespoons freshly squeezed lime juice
- ¼ cup chopped fresh cilantro, plus ¼ cup
- 4 garlic cloves, minced, plus 4 cloves minced
- ¼ teaspoon salt, plus ¼ teaspoon
- ¼ teaspoon crushed red pepper flakes, plus ¼ teaspoon
- 2 tablespoons coconut oil

1. In a large nonreactive (glass or ceramic) bowl, add the shrimp and the lime juice, ¼ cup of cilantro, 4 cloves of garlic, ¼ teaspoon of salt, and ¼ teaspoon of red pepper flakes, and toss to mix well. Cover and refrigerate for about 20 minutes.

2. Heat the coconut oil in a large, heavy skillet over medium-high heat. When the oil is very hot, add the shrimp, along with the marinade and the remaining 4 cloves garlic. Cook, stirring frequently, for about 5 minutes, until the shrimp are pink and cooked through. Remove from the heat and stir in the remaining ¼ cup cilantro, ¼ teaspoon salt, and ¼ teaspoon red pepper flakes.

3. Serve immediately.

Shrimp Dumplings in Cabbage Leaf Wrappers

SERVES 4   PREP TIME: 15 MINUTES   COOK TIME: 15 MINUTES

● ● ●   *Most dumplings come in wrappers made with refined flour, but these use steamed cabbage leaves to hold their flavorful filling of plump shrimp spiked with ginger, garlic, and aromatic vegetables. The usual wheat-containing soy sauce is replaced by a simple dipping sauce using coconut aminos instead.*

1 head Napa cabbage, leaves separated
1 tablespoon coconut oil
1 celery stalk, minced
½ small onion, minced
½ small carrot, shredded
2 tablespoons coconut aminos
¼ teaspoon salt
¼ teaspoon freshly ground black pepper
¼ teaspoon fish sauce, plus ¼ teaspoon
¼ cup sliced scallions, plus 2 tablespoons
1 pound shrimp, peeled and deveined, minced
1 teaspoon minced fresh ginger
1 garlic clove, minced
¼ cup coconut aminos
2 tablespoons sesame oil
2 teaspoons rice vinegar
1 tablespoon freshly squeezed lime juice

1. Fill a large pot fitted with a steamer basket with 1 inch of water, and bring to a boil. Add all but 2 of the cabbage leaves to the pot, cover, and steam for about 5 minutes, until the leaves become pliable. Remove the leaves from the pot and set aside. ▶

2. To make the filling, julienne the remaining 2 cabbage leaves. Heat the coconut oil in a large skillet over medium heat, and add the julienned cabbage, celery, onion, carrot, coconut aminos, salt, pepper, and ¼ teaspoon of the fish sauce. Cook, stirring frequently, for about 5 minutes, until the vegetables are soft. Stir in ¼ cup of the scallions.

3. Add the shrimp, ginger, and garlic, and cook, stirring and breaking up the shrimp with a spatula, for about 3 minutes, until the shrimp are cooked through.

4. To fill the dumplings, lay a steamed cabbage leaf on the work surface, and place about 2 tablespoons of the filling in the center. Fold the sides and ends of the leaf over the filling, and roll until completely wrapped. Secure the dumpling with a toothpick. Continue making dumplings with the remaining cabbage leaves and filling.

5. To make the dipping sauce, in a small bowl, whisk together the coconut aminos, sesame oil, vinegar, lime juice, and the remaining ¼ teaspoon fish sauce until well combined. Stir in the remaining 2 tablespoons scallions.

6. Serve the dumplings warm with small bowls of the sauce alongside for dipping.

Indian Butter Scallops

SERVES 4   PREP TIME: 10 MINUTES   COOK TIME: 15 MINUTES

A riff on the classic Indian dish called butter chicken, this seafood version uses the same rich, creamy, spiced tomato sauce, but includes quick-cooking scallops. Serve this luxurious dish over Cauliflower "Rice" (page 372).

2 tablespoons ghee (clarified butter) or butter

½ cup minced shallot

2 garlic cloves, minced

2 teaspoons minced peeled fresh ginger

¼ cup tomato paste

½ teaspoon salt

2 teaspoons garam masala

⅛ teaspoon cayenne pepper

¼ teaspoon ground cumin

¼ teaspoon ground cinnamon

1 pound sea scallops

1 cup heavy cream

2 tablespoons chopped cilantro, for garnish

1. Heat the ghee in a large skillet over medium-high heat. Add the shallot and cook, stirring frequently, about 3 minutes, until it begins to soften. Stir in the garlic, ginger, tomato paste, salt, garam masala, cayenne pepper, cumin, and cinnamon. Cook, stirring frequently, for 3 minutes.

2. Add the scallops and cream and cook for about 5 minutes, stirring occasionally, until the scallops are cooked through. Serve immediately, garnished with cilantro.

Mussels Steamed in Coconut Milk

SERVES 4   PREP TIME: 10 MINUTES   COOK TIME: 15 MINUTES

Mussels are inexpensive and easy to prepare but are often overlooked as a protein option. Here they're simmered in a spicy bath of coconut milk and lime juice. The mussels themselves are plump and satisfying, but you'll want a spoon to slurp up every bit of the flavorful broth, as well.

2 pounds mussels

1½ cups coconut milk

1 red bell pepper, diced

2 cups diced tomatoes

½ cup chopped fresh cilantro

2 jalapeño chiles, halved and seeded

Zest and juice of 1 lime

2 tablespoons fresh oregano or 2 teaspoons dried oregano

½ teaspoon salt

¼ teaspoon freshly ground pepper

1. Rinse the mussels well, pull off the beards and discard any mussels that have broken shells or remain open when tapped.

2. In a medium stockpot, heat the coconut milk over medium-high heat. Add the bell pepper, tomatoes, cilantro, jalapeño chiles, lime zest, lime juice, fresh oregano, salt, and pepper, and bring to a simmer.

3. Add the mussels, stir, cover, reduce the heat to medium-low, and simmer for about 5 minutes, until the mussels have opened. Discard any mussels that haven't opened. ▶

4. To serve, divide the mussels evenly among 4 bowls, then ladle some of the broth over each serving. Serve hot.

TIP   Always check mussels before cooking to make sure their shells are closed, which means they are still alive. If a shell is open, give it a few taps. If it remains open, that's a sure sign that you should discard it. Likewise, if a mussel doesn't open during cooking, toss it.

Seared Sea Scallops with Bacon and Kale

SERVES 4   PREP TIME: 5 MINUTES   COOK TIME: 12 MINUTES

● ● ● *Luscious sea scallops and crisp, smoky bacon are a classic combination that always makes for a success. Sautéed kale flavored with fresh basil and chives makes a nutritious base for the dish, though you can substitute spinach, chard, or another leafy green for the kale, if desired.*

½ pound bacon, diced

3 medium shallots, diced

12 large sea scallops

1 bunch kale leaves, tough center ribs removed, leaves julienned

1 tablespoon chopped fresh basil, for garnish

1 tablespoon chopped fresh chives, for garnish

1. Cook the bacon strips in a large skillet over medium-high heat for about 3 minutes on each side, until browned and crisp. Add the shallots and cook, stirring frequently, for about 5 minutes, until the shallots are softened. Add the kale and cook, stirring frequently, for about 5 minutes, until tender. Transfer the kale mixture to a bowl and set aside.

2. Add the scallops to the pan with the bacon fat, and cook for about 3 minutes, until golden brown on the bottom. Turn the scallops over and cook for about 3 minutes, until nicely browned on the other side. Transfer the scallops to a warm plate.

3. Return the kale mixture to the pan, and cook for 1 to 2 minutes, until heated through. ▶

4. Serve the scallops hot on top of the kale mixture, garnished with the basil and chives.

TIP   Scallops are easy to overcook and when this happens, they become tough and chewy. To avoid this, cook them in a very hot pan over medium-hot heat, turning them just once, until they have a golden-brown crust and have just turned opaque throughout.

Thai Shrimp Curry

SERVES 4   PREP TIME: 10 MINUTES   COOK TIME: 15 MINUTES

● ● ●   *This is a particularly easy recipe that's endlessly flexible. Don't want to splurge on prawns? Use chicken instead. Don't have broccoli? Substitute cauliflower or zucchini. Don't like cilantro? The dish would be just as tasty using fresh basil. This dish is loaded with vegetables, making it a fantastic one-pot meal, but a side of cauliflower "rice" would be a welcome addition.*

1 shallot
3 garlic cloves
1-inch piece of ginger, peeled and cut in half
1 to 2 tablespoons Thai red curry paste
3 tablespoons fish sauce
2 kaffir lime leaves or 1 teaspoon fresh lime zest
1 (13½-ounce) can coconut milk
1 tablespoon tomato paste
1 tablespoon coconut oil
2 medium carrots, diced
1 head broccoli, cut into small florets
1 red bell pepper, seeded and diced
1 pound peeled and deveined prawns
½ cup chopped fresh cilantro
Juice of ½ lime

1. In a food processor or blender, add the shallot, garlic, ginger, curry paste, and fish sauce, and pulse to a paste.

2. Transfer the mixture to a large stockpot and add the kaffir leaves, coconut milk, tomato paste, and coconut oil. Bring to a boil over medium-high heat and cook, stirring frequently, for about 10 minutes. ▶

3. Reduce the heat to medium-low, and add the carrots, broccoli, and bell pepper. Cook for 6 to 8 minutes, until the vegetables are tender. Add the prawns and cook for about 3 minutes, until the shrimp are pink and cooked through.

4. Just before serving, stir in the cilantro and lime juice. Serve hot.

Calamari in Saffron Tomato Broth

SERVES 4 PREP TIME: 5 MINUTES COOK TIME: 50 MINUTES

● ● ● *A fine example of Spanish cuisine, this calamari dish is braised in a light broth flavored with tomato and saffron. The end result is light yet surprisingly elegant and makes a perfect meal on a warm evening. Serve this dish with a crisp green salad dressed with a citrus vinaigrette.*

- 3 tablespoons olive oil
- 2 garlic cloves, minced
- 1 onion, diced
- ¼ teaspoon salt, plus ¼ teaspoon
- 1 medium tomato, grated
- 2 pounds calamari rings
- ½ teaspoon sweet paprika
- 6 saffron threads
- 1 cup white wine
- 2 tablespoons chopped fresh flat-leaf parsley

1. Heat the olive oil in a large saucepan over medium-high heat. Add the garlic, onion, and ¼ teaspoon of the salt. Reduce the heat to low and cook, stirring occasionally, for 10 minutes. Stir in the tomato and continue to cook for 5 minutes. ▶

2. Raise the heat to medium, add the calamari, and cook for 3 minutes, stirring. Add the remaining ¼ teaspoon of salt, the sweet paprika, and the saffron threads, crumbling the threads into the pot with your fingers. Add the wine and stir. Cover the pot and simmer for about 30 minutes, until the calamari is tender.

3. Serve hot, garnished with parsley.

> TIP   Although alcoholic beverages are prohibited on the sugar detox diet, using a bit of wine in cooking is allowed since the sugar-containing alcohol evaporates during cooking and wine gives a distinctive flavor to a dish. But if you'd rather not have wine around during your detox, you can simply substitute chicken or vegetable broth.

Simple Salmon Cakes

SERVES 4 TO 6   PREP TIME: 5 MINUTES   COOK TIME: 15 MINUTES

● ● ●   *These salmon cakes are seasoned with Japanese ume plum vinegar, a bracing concoction infused with the flavor of Japanese umeboshi plums. Serve these cakes on a bed of lettuce with a squeeze of lemon, accompanied by a crisp green salad.*

1 pound skinless salmon fillets, diced

1 tablespoon sesame oil

1 tablespoon ume plum vinegar

1 teaspoon minced garlic

1 teaspoon minced peeled fresh ginger

¼ cup diced red onion

2 eggs, lightly beaten

1 tablespoon almond meal

1 tablespoon olive oil

1. In a medium bowl, with a wooden spoon or your hands, mix together the diced salmon, sesame oil, vinegar, garlic, ginger, onion, and eggs. Add the almond meal and mix well.

2. Shape the mixture into patties using a ¼-cup measure.

3. Heat the olive oil in a heavy medium skillet over medium-high heat. Add the patties to the skillet and cook for 4 to 6 minutes on each side, until lightly browned. Cook in two batches if necessary. Drain the patties on a paper towel–lined plate, and repeat with the remaining salmon mixture.

4. Serve hot.

TIP   Ume plum vinegar, also called umeboshi vinegar, is a little fruity and quite salty. If you can't find it, substitute red wine vinegar mixed with a little salt or coconut aminos.

Classic Old Bay–Seasoned Crab Cakes

SERVES 4   PREP TIME: 10 MINUTES   COOK TIME 25 MINUTES

● ● ●   *Crab cakes are usually loaded with bread crumbs, but these are grain free. Held together with an egg and a bit of Homemade Mayonnaise, they're full of plump crabmeat without all the fillers. The quintessential crab cake seasoning mix, Old Bay, gives them their classic flavor.*

1 pound lump crabmeat

1 egg, lightly beaten

2 tablespoons Homemade Mayonnaise (page 364)

1 medium shallot, minced

1 tablespoon chopped flat-leaf parsley

1 tablespoon Old Bay seasoning

½ teaspoon salt

1. Preheat the oven to 350°F. Line a large baking sheet with parchment paper.

2. In a large mixing bowl, stir together the crabmeat, egg, Homemade Mayonnaise, shallot, parsley, Old Bay seasoning, and salt.

3. Form the crab mixture into patties using about ¼ cup of the mixture for each and place them on the prepared baking sheet.

4. Bake the crab cakes for about 25 minutes, until they are lightly browned and beginning to crisp on the outside. Serve hot.

Shrimp and Sausage Gumbo

SERVES 4 PREP TIME: 10 MINUTES COOK TIME: 35 MINUTES

Gumbo is the traditional Creole soup. This version includes plump shrimp and smoky andouille chicken sausage in a hearty broth full of vegetables. It's a filling soup on its own, but if you'd like some extra substance, serve it enriched with a scoop of Cauliflower "Rice" (page 372).

2 tablespoons olive oil

1 onion, diced

3 stalks celery, diced

1 red bell pepper, diced

1 green bell pepper, diced

3 garlic cloves, minced

2 tablespoons tomato paste

2 teaspoons paprika

1 teaspoon dried thyme

1 teaspoon dried oregano

½ teaspoon cayenne pepper

1 teaspoon salt

½ teaspoon freshly ground black pepper

6 cups chicken broth

2 bay leaves

4 links andouille chicken sausages, sliced

1½ pounds peeled and deveined shrimp

2 tablespoons chopped fresh flat-leaf parsley, for garnish

1. Heat the oil in a large stockpot over medium heat. Add the onion, celery, red bell pepper, green bell pepper, and garlic, and cook, stirring frequently, for about 5 minutes, until the onions are softened.

2. Stir in the tomato paste, paprika, thyme, oregano, cayenne pepper, salt, and black pepper and cook, stirring, for 30 seconds. Add the chicken broth and bay leaves, and bring to a boil. Reduce the heat to medium-low and simmer for 10 minutes.

3. Add the sausage and simmer for 5 minutes. Add the shrimp and cook for about 5 minutes, until the shrimp is just cooked through.

4. Serve hot, garnished with parsley.

Baked Mahimahi with Cilantro Garlic Sauce

SERVES 4   PREP TIME: 5 MINUTES   COOK TIME: 25 MINUTES

● ● ● *Mahimahi is a firm-fleshed, meaty, and slightly sweet-flavored fish. Baking it in an herb sauce of cilantro and garlic keeps it moist and infuses it with flavor. This dish takes only a few minutes to put together, then you just stick it in the oven to bake while you make a salad or set the table, and you're good to go!*

2 tablespoons olive oil, plus more for the baking dish

⅔ cup chopped fresh cilantro

½ cup chicken broth

4 garlic cloves

1 tablespoon coconut aminos

½ teaspoon salt

¼ teaspoon freshly ground black pepper

4 (6-ounce) mahimahi fillets

1. Preheat the oven to 375°F. Brush a large baking dish with olive oil.

2. In a food processor or blender, add the cilantro, chicken broth, garlic, coconut aminos, salt, and pepper, and purée until smooth.

3. Place the fish in a single layer in the baking dish, and pour the sauce over the fillets.

4. Bake for 20 to 25 minutes, until the fish is cooked through and flakes easily with a fork. Serve immediately.

Pan-Fried Trout with Cherry Tomatoes and Bacon

SERVES 4   PREP TIME: 5 MINUTES   COOK TIME: 15 MINUTES

● ● ●   *This simple, elegant meal—delicate trout cooked in bacon fat with fragrant thyme, bright, juicy cherry tomatoes, and a crumble of crispy bacon—can be ready in less than 20 minutes. To save time and effort, buy trout fillets, and this recipe will be a breeze. A green salad or roasted vegetables is all you need to round out the meal.*

4 slices bacon

1 pint cherry tomatoes, halved

1 garlic clove, minced

½ teaspoon salt, plus ½ teaspoon

½ teaspoon freshly ground black pepper, plus ½ teaspoon

1 tablespoon minced fresh thyme

Cooking spray for the pan

4 (6-ounce) trout fillets

1 lemon, cut into 4 wedges

1. Heat a medium skillet over medium-high heat. Add the bacon and cook for 6 minutes, turning once, until crisp. Transfer the bacon strips to a paper towel–lined plate to drain, then crumble them. Drain off all but 1 tablespoon of the bacon fat from the pan.

2. Add the cherry tomatoes, garlic, ½ teaspoon of salt, and ½ teaspoon of pepper to the skillet, and cook, stirring, for about 3 minutes, until the tomatoes just begin to break down. Remove from the heat and stir in the crumbled bacon and thyme. ▶

3. Spray a large nonstick skillet with cooking spray and heat it over medium-high heat. Sprinkle the fish fillets with the remaining ½ teaspoon of salt and ½ teaspoon of pepper, and add them to the pan (you may need to cook the fish in two batches to avoid over-crowding). Cook the fish, turning once, for 2 to 3 minutes per side, until it is cooked through and flakes easily with a fork.

4. Transfer the fillets to 4 serving plates, and top with the tomato mixture. Serve immediately with a lemon wedge.

Lettuce-Wrapped Fish Tacos

SERVES 4   PREP TIME: 10 MINUTES   COOK TIME: 5 MINUTES

● ● ●   *Coated with spices and almond meal and fried in coconut oil, strips of quick-cooking white fish make a perfect crispy filling for lettuce-wrapped tacos. Add a dollop of your favorite salsa and a drizzle of mayonnaise spiked with lime juice and spices, and you have a fiesta!*

FOR THE SAUCE

½ cup Homemade Mayonnaise (page 364)
1 tablespoon freshly squeezed lime juice
1 teaspoon dried oregano
½ teaspoon ground cumin
¼ teaspoon of chili powder

FOR THE FISH

½ cup almond meal
1 tablespoon garlic powder
2 teaspoons ground cumin
2 teaspoons salt
½ teaspoon freshly ground black pepper
1 pound white fish fillets (such as cod or halibut),
    cut into ½-by-3-inch strips
Coconut oil for frying

TO SERVE

8 large lettuce leaves
1 cup salsa
2 tablespoons chopped cilantro
2 limes, cut into 8 wedges

1. To make the sauce, in a small bowl, add the Homemade Mayonnaise, lime juice, oregano, cumin, and chili powder, and stir to mix well. ▶

2. To prepare the fish, in a shallow dish, add the almond meal, garlic powder, cumin, salt, and pepper, and stir to mix well. Dredge the fish in the almond meal mixture to coat well.

3. Fill a wide saucepan with about ½ inch of coconut oil and heat over high heat. When the oil is hot, carefully add the fish. Cook for about 5 minutes, turning once, until the coating is golden brown on both sides. Transfer the fish pieces to a paper towel–lined plate to drain.

4. To serve, place 2 lettuce leaves on each of 4 serving plates. Top each leaf with a few pieces of fish, a dollop of salsa, and a drizzle of the sauce. Garnish with cilantro, and serve each with a lime wedge.

Baked Salmon with Caramelized Leeks

SERVES 4   PREP TIME: 5 MINUTES   COOK TIME: 40 MINUTES

● ● ●   *In this extremely simple dish, flaky roasted salmon is topped with melt-in-your-mouth, slow-cooked leeks that have been caramelized to bring out their sweetness. Serve with Braised Brussels Sprouts with Shallots and Thyme (page 203), or Spiced Broccoli with Toasted Coconut (page 206), for a complete, satisfying meal. If you're on the blue plan, just replace the butter with coconut oil.*

Cooking spray for the pan

1 tablespoon butter or coconut oil

2 leeks (white and light green parts) halved lengthwise, thinly sliced, and rinsed

¼ teaspoon salt, plus ¼ teaspoon

½ teaspoon freshly squeezed lemon juice

4 (6-ounce) wild salmon fillets

¼ teaspoon freshly ground black pepper

⅛ teaspoon cayenne pepper

1. Preheat the oven to 400°F. Coat a large rimmed baking sheet with cooking spray.

2. Set a large nonstick skillet over medium heat. Add the butter and leeks to the skillet and cook, stirring occasionally, for about 5 minutes, until the leeks are softened. Stir in ¼ teaspoon of salt, reduce the heat to low, and cook, stirring occasionally, for about 20 minutes, until the leeks are browned and very soft. Remove the pan from the heat, and stir in the lemon juice.

3. Meanwhile, place the salmon on the prepared baking sheet, and season with the remaining ¼ teaspoon salt, black pepper, and cayenne pepper. Bake for 10 to 12 minutes, until the fish is cooked through and flakes easily with a fork. Serve the salmon topped with the leeks.

Baked Salmon with Cherry Tomato and Avocado Salsa

SERVES 4   PREP TIME: 10 MINUTES   COOK TIME: 8 MINUTES

● ● ●   *A simple salsa of cherry tomatoes and avocado dresses up seared salmon fillets for a quick, fresh, and healthy meal you can bring to the table in less than 20 minutes. Serve with a green salad or Sautéed Chard with Shiitakes and Garlic (page 207).*

Coconut oil, for greasing the pan

4 (6-ounce) wild salmon fillets

¾ teaspoon salt, plus ½ teaspoon

½ teaspoon freshly ground black pepper, plus ¼ teaspoon

1 pint cherry tomatoes, quartered

2 scallions, thinly sliced

1 medium avocado, diced

1 large jalapeño chile, seeded and minced

¼ cup minced fresh cilantro

2 tablespoons olive oil

Juice of 1 lime

1. Preheat the oven to 400°F and coat a baking dish with coconut oil.

2. Season the salmon on both sides with ½ teaspoon of salt and ¼ teaspoon of pepper. Bake the salmon for 10 to 15 minutes, until the salmon is cooked through. ▶

3. While the salmon is cooking, make the salsa. In a medium bowl, combine the tomatoes, scallions, avocado, jalapeño, cilantro, olive oil, lime juice, the remaining ¾ teaspoon of salt, and the remaining ½ teaspoon of pepper, and stir to mix well. Set aside.

4. Serve the salmon immediately, topped with a generous spoonful of salsa.

Cod Baked with Tomato Sauce and Olives

SERVES 4   PREP TIME: 5 MINUTES   COOK TIME: 50 MINUTES

Cod is a meaty, mild white fish that's easy to cook and pairs well with many other flavors. Here it's baked in a rich tomato sauce spiked with fresh garlic and basil, and studded with salty, pungent olives and capers for a Mediterranean flavor.

2 tablespoons olive oil

3 garlic cloves, minced

1 bunch fresh basil, leaves and stems separated, leaves chopped and stems minced

1 red jalapeño chile, halved and seeded

1 (28-ounce) can diced tomatoes with their juice

1 teaspoon salt, plus more for the fish

½ teaspoon freshly ground black pepper, plus more for the fish

1 tablespoon red wine vinegar

4 (6-ounce) cod fillets

½ cup pitted, oil-cured black olives

1 tablespoon capers, drained

1. Heat the olive oil in a large skillet over medium heat. Add the garlic, basil stems, and jalapeño chile and cook, stirring frequently, for about 3 minutes, until the garlic is softened.

2. Add the tomatoes, salt, and pepper. Bring to a boil, reduce the heat to medium-low, and simmer for about 30 minutes. Remove from the heat, and discard the chile halves. Stir in the vinegar.

3. Preheat the oven to 425°F. ▶

4. Pour the tomato sauce into a 9-by-11-inch baking dish. Season the fillets with salt and pepper, and place them on top of the sauce. Scatter the olives, capers, and the remaining basil leaves on top.

5. Bake for about 15 minutes, until the fish is cooked through and flakes easily with a fork. Serve immediately.

Halibut with Almond-Mustard Crust

SERVES 4   PREP TIME: 5 MINUTES   COOK TIME: 10 MINUTES

● ● ●   *This recipe turns a mild fillet of fish into a flavorful and elegant meal. With just a handful of ingredients, a zesty crust of mustard and ground almonds adds both crunch and flavor. Serve this dish with sautéed greens, roasted vegetables, or a green salad for a complete meal.*

½ cup coarsely ground almond meal

4 (6-ounce) halibut fillets

1 teaspoon minced fresh thyme

¾ teaspoon salt

½ teaspoon freshly ground black pepper

½ cup Dijon mustard

2 tablespoons coconut oil

2 tablespoons chopped fresh flat-leaf parsley, for garnish

1 lemon, cut into 4 wedges, for garnish

1. Place the almond meal in a wide, shallow dish.

2. Season the fish on both sides with the thyme, salt, and pepper. Coat both sides of each fillet with the mustard, then press the fillet into the almond meal to coat well.

3. Heat the coconut oil in a large skillet over medium-high heat. Add the fish and cook for 3 minutes per side, until lightly browned and cooked through. Serve immediately, garnished with parsley and lemon wedges.

Baked Cod with Lemon and Herbs

SERVES 4   PREP TIME: 5 MINUTES   COOK TIME: 20 MINUTES

● ● ●   *This straightforward recipe allows fresh cod to really shine. If cod isn't available, you can substitute other white fish such as halibut or snapper. Serve it alongside roasted broccoli or Braised Brussels Sprouts with Shallots and Thyme (page 203).*

4 (6-ounce) cod fillets

1½ tablespoons freshly squeezed lemon juice

1 tablespoon olive oil

2 garlic cloves, minced

1 teaspoon minced fresh thyme

1 teaspoon salt

½ teaspoon freshly ground black pepper

2 tablespoons chopped fresh flat-leaf parsley, for garnish

1. Preheat the oven to 400°F.

2. Arrange the fish fillets in a 9-by-13-inch baking dish. Over the top of the fish, sprinkle the lemon juice, olive oil, garlic, thyme, salt, and pepper.

3. Bake the fillets for 15 to 20 minutes, until the fish is opaque and flakes easily with a fork. Serve immediately, garnished with the parsley.

Seared Ahi Tuna with Wasabi Aioli

SERVES 4
PREP TIME: 5 MINUTES, PLUS 30 MINUTES TO MARINATE THE FISH
COOK TIME: 6 MINUTES

● ● ●   *Seared ahi tuna is satisfyingly meaty and very simple to prepare. The key to succulent tuna is to cook it in a very hot pan until the surface of the fish is seared to a light brown but the center is still pink and succulent.*

2 tablespoons peeled minced fresh ginger

2 tablespoons sesame oil

2 teaspoons crushed red pepper flakes

Juice of 1 lime

½ teaspoon fish sauce

1 tablespoon coconut aminos

4 (6-ounce) sushi-grade ahi tuna steaks

½ cup Homemade Mayonnaise (page 364)

1 tablespoon wasabi paste

1 tablespoon coconut oil

1. In a small bowl, whisk together the ginger, sesame oil, red pepper flakes, lime juice, fish sauce, and coconut aminos.

2. Place the tuna steaks in a glass or ceramic baking dish, and pour the marinade over them. Turn the fish to coat, then cover and refrigerate for about 30 minutes.

3. Meanwhile, make the aioli by stirring together the Homemade Mayonnaise and wasabi paste in a small bowl.

4. Heat the coconut oil in a large, heavy skillet over high heat. Add the tuna steaks to the pan and cook for about 3 minutes per side, until the surface is lightly browned but the center of the fish is still raw. Remove from the pan to a cutting board and let rest for a few minutes. Slice thinly and serve drizzled with the aioli.

TIP   Because the fish isn't cooked all the way through, it's important to use only sushi-grade tuna for this dish.

Stir-Fried Sole with Chiles and Garlic

SERVES 4
**PREP TIME: 5 MINUTES (PLUS 30 MINUTES
TO SOAK THE CHILES AND I HOUR TO MARINATE THE FISH)**
COOK TIME: I0 MINUTES

● ● ●   *Sole is a delicate fish ideal for pan-searing. Here it's marinated in a rich paste of red chiles and garlic with a dash of vinegar. Serve this dish atop Cauliflower "Rice" (page 372), if desired.*

3 to 4 dried red chiles, soaked in hot water for 30 minutes and drained

6 garlic cloves

½ teaspoon salt

2 tablespoons rice vinegar

1 tablespoon plus 1 teaspoon coconut oil, divided

1½ pounds fillet of sole, cut into bite-size pieces

1 onion, thinly sliced

2 tablespoons chicken broth or water

2 tablespoons chopped cilantro, for garnish

1. In a food processor or blender, add the chiles, garlic, salt, vinegar, and 1 teaspoon of the coconut oil, and process to a paste.

2. Rub the chile-garlic paste all over the fish, put on a plate, and refrigerate for 1 hour.

3. Heat the remaining 1 tablespoon coconut oil in a large skillet over medium-high heat. Add the fish to the pan, reserving the marinating liquid, and cook for 2 to 3 minutes per side, until golden brown. Transfer the fish to a serving platter.

4. Add the onion and the reserved marinade to the pan and cook, stirring, for 1 minute. Add the chicken broth and cook, stirring frequently, until the onions are softened, for about 5 minutes.

5. Spoon the onion mixture over the fish and serve immediately, garnished with cilantro.

TIP   If possible, choose wild sole from the Pacific Ocean, which is more sustainable than Atlantic sole.

Seafood Stew with Garlic Aioli

SERVES 4   PREP TIME: I0 MINUTES   COOK TIME: 25 MINUTES

Seafood stew is easy to make but always impressive. Loaded with clams, shrimp, and red snapper, this tomato-flavored version makes an elegant party dish or a quick supper. A dollop of garlic aioli, made with Homemade Mayonnaise, takes it over the top.

FOR THE STEW

2 tablespoons olive oil

1 large shallot, thinly sliced

2 garlic cloves, minced, plus 2 cloves minced

½ cup dry white wine

1½ cups chicken broth

1 cup bottled clam juice

1 cup drained, diced tomatoes (15-ounce can)

2 thyme sprigs

1 bay leaf

½ teaspoon hot pepper sauce, plus more for serving

1 teaspoon salt

½ teaspoon freshly ground black pepper

2 dozen littleneck clams, scrubbed

¾ pound skinless snapper fillets, cut into 2-inch pieces

½ pound peeled and deveined medium shrimp

2 tablespoons coarsely chopped flat-leaf parsley, for garnish

FOR THE AIOLI

½ cup Homemade Mayonnaise (page 364)

1. Heat the olive oil in a large stockpot over medium-high heat. Add the shallot and 2 cloves of garlic and cook, stirring frequently, for about 5 minutes, until the shallots are softened. Stir in the wine and bring to a boil. Cook for about 3 minutes, until the liquid is reduced by about half. Add the chicken broth, clam juice, tomatoes, thyme, bay leaf, hot pepper sauce, salt, and pepper. Raise the heat to high and bring to a boil. Let cook for about 10 minutes, until the liquid is slightly reduced.

2. Stir in the clams, cover, and cook for about 5 minutes, until the clams have opened. Add the snapper and shrimp, cover, and cook for about 3 minutes, until the fish and shrimp are cooked through and all the clams have opened (discard any clams that haven't opened).

3. To make the aioli, stir together the Homemade Mayonnaise and the remaining 2 cloves garlic in a small bowl.

4. To serve, use a slotted spoon to divide the seafood among 4 serving bowls. Ladle the broth into each bowl, and serve garnished with a dollop of aioli and a sprinkling of parsley.

TWELVE

POULTRY

Spice-Rubbed Grilled Chicken Thighs

SERVES 4 TO 6   PREP TIME: 5 MINUTES   COOK TIME: 30 MINUTES

● ● ●   *Spice rubs are a great way to add quick flavor to meats before grilling. This version combines the flavors of garlic, onions, chili powder, and oregano for a fragrant kick. All you need to round out this meal is a crisp salad with vinaigrette dressing.*

1 teaspoon garlic powder
1 teaspoon onion powder
1 teaspoon dried oregano
½ teaspoon ground turmeric
½ teaspoon chili powder
½ teaspoon paprika
½ teaspoon salt
¼ teaspoon freshly ground black pepper
8 bone-in, skin-on chicken thighs

1. Preheat the grill to medium heat.

2. In a small bowl, stir together the garlic powder, onion powder, oregano, turmeric, chili powder, paprika, salt, and pepper.

3. Pat the chicken thighs dry, and coat the skin liberally with the spice mixture.

4. Cook the chicken skin-side up for 25 to 30 minutes, until cooked through. Turn the chicken pieces over, and cook for 1 to 2 minutes on the skin side to crisp.

5. Serve immediately.

TIP   Make some extra spice rub, and save it in a jar in your spice cupboard for those evenings when you just want to throw something on the grill for dinner. It works equally well with fish or steak.

Grilled Bacon-Stuffed Chicken Pinwheels

SERVES 4 TO 6   PREP TIME: 15 MINUTES   COOK TIME: 15 MINUTES

● ● ●   *Stuffing chicken breast fillets with bacon, rolling them into pinwheels, and skewering them to cook on the grill is a fun but simple way to make grilled chicken particularly interesting. Adding fresh spinach, basil, and garlic adds flavor and keeps the chicken moist.*

> 4 strips bacon
> 2 pounds boneless skinless chicken breast
> 2 garlic cloves, minced
> 1 cup julienned fresh spinach leaves
> ¼ cup chopped fresh basil

1. Soak several bamboo skewers in water for 30 minutes.

2. Heat a medium skillet over medium-high heat. Add the bacon and cook for 2 to 3 minutes, until it is beginning to brown but still pliable. Remove from the pan and drain on paper towels.

3. Place a sheet of plastic wrap on the work surface. Cut the chicken breasts in half horizontally to make 2 thin fillets out of each. Lay the fillets side by side and top with a second piece of plastic wrap. Using a mallet, pound each fillet until it is about ¼-inch thick. Repeat with the remaining fillets.

4. Spread the garlic over one side of each of the fillets, dividing equally. Arrange the bacon slices on each of the chicken pieces, dividing them equally. Similarly divide the spinach and basil over the chicken fillets. ▶

5. Roll up each chicken fillet tightly around the filling and cut the roles into 2-inch wide slices. Place 3 rounds in a row, and push a skewer through them crosswise to hold them together. Repeat with all of the pinwheels.

6. Heat a grill or grill pan to medium heat, and cook the pinwheels for about 5 minutes per side, until the chicken is cooked through. Serve immediately.

Chicken Breast Stir-Fry with Zucchini, Bell Peppers, and Pea Shoots

---

SERVES 4   PREP TIME: 5 MINUTES   COOK TIME: 20 MINUTES

A quick stir-fry is one of the best ways to get a healthy dinner on the table in a hurry. This one is full of vegetables—red bell pepper, onion, zucchini, and pea shoots—and seasoned with coconut aminos in place of soy sauce. Pea shoots add a pleasing delicate green. If you can't find fresh pea shoots, usually available in spring, substitute an equal quantity of baby spinach leaves.

   2 tablespoons coconut oil
   2 large chicken breasts, cut into 1-inch pieces
   1 onion, diced
   1 red bell pepper, seeded and diced
   1 zucchini, cut into small dice
   1 tablespoon coconut aminos
   2 cups pea shoots

1. Heat the coconut oil in a large heavy skillet over medium-high heat. Add the chicken and cook, stirring frequently, for about 5 minutes, until browned.

2. Add the onion and bell pepper, and cook for about 5 minutes, until the vegetables begin to soften.

3. Add the zucchini and continue to cook, stirring frequently, for about 5 minutes, until the vegetables are softened and nicely browned. ▶

4. Stir in the coconut aminos.

5. Add the pea shoots and cook, stirring, for about 2 minutes, just until the pea shoots wilt. Serve immediately.

Tandoori-Spiced Chicken Breast

SERVES 4

PREP TIME: 15 MINUTES (PLUS 2 TO 24 HOURS TO MARINATE THE CHICKEN)

COOK TIME: 30 MINUTES

Though chicken breast can sometimes turn out dry and bland, in this dish, enzymes from the yogurt in the marinade for this flavorful Indian specialty makes the chicken extremely tender. The marinade is then discarded, so it hardly adds any carbohydrates to the finished dish.

2 cups plain yogurt

1½ tablespoons grated peeled fresh ginger

2 tablespoons olive oil, plus more for the pan

1½ teaspoons ground cumin

¾ teaspoon cayenne pepper

2 garlic cloves, minced

1½ pounds skinless, boneless chicken breast

1 teaspoon salt

1. In a large bowl or resealable plastic bag, add the yogurt, ginger, olive oil, cumin, cayenne pepper, and garlic, and stir to combine. Add the chicken and toss to coat, then marinate in the refrigerator for at least 2 hours or as long as all day or overnight.

2. Preheat oven to 400°F. Lightly coat a roasting pan with olive oil.

3. Remove the chicken from the marinade, and discard the marinade. Season the chicken on both sides with the salt, and place it in a single layer in the prepared roasting pan. Bake for about 30 minutes, turning once, until browned and cooked through.

4. Serve hot.

Tangy Chicken Piccata

SERVES 4   PREP TIME: 10 MINUTES   COOK TIME: 15 MINUTES

● ● ●   *In this classic Italian dish, the chicken is normally dredged in flour. Here, almond meal stands in for the flour, and the chicken is bathed in the traditional lemony sauce studded with capers and garnished with parsley.*

2 boneless, skinless chicken breasts

1 egg

2 tablespoons water

½ cup almond meal

1 teaspoon salt

½ teaspoon freshly ground black pepper

¼ teaspoon cayenne pepper

1 tablespoon coconut oil

Juice of 1 freshly squeezed lemon

½ cup white wine

1 tablespoon capers, drained

1 tablespoon minced fresh flat-leaf parsley

1. Preheat the oven to 400°F.

2. Halve the chicken breasts horizontally so that you have two thin filets from each. Pound the chicken between two pieces of plastic wrap to a thinkness of ¼ inch.

3. In a shallow bowl, whisk together the egg and water.

4. In another shallow bowl, add the almond meal, salt, black pepper, and cayenne pepper and stir to combine.

5. Heat the coconut oil in a large, oven-safe skillet over medium-high heat.

6. Dredge the chicken first in the egg and then in the almond meal mixture. ▶

7. Add the chicken to the skillet and cook for about 3 minutes, until the bottom is nicely browned. Turn the chicken over and cook the other side for about 3 minutes, until golden brown.

8. Transfer the skillet to the oven, and bake for about 5 minutes, until cooked through.

9. Transfer the chicken to serving plates. Over medium heat, deglaze the skillet with the lemon juice and wine over medium heat, stirring with a wooden spoon to release the flavorful brown bits on the bottom. Simmer for about 2 minutes, until the sauce is reduced by about half. Stir in the capers. Spoon the sauce over the chicken breasts. Serve immediately, garnished with the parsley.

Prosciutto-Wrapped Chicken Stuffed with Goat Cheese

SERVES 4   PREP TIME: 15 MINUTES   COOK TIME: 25 MINUTES

Though it's easily prepared, this chicken dish offers an air of elegance. It's a great dinner party option since all the prep can be done ahead of time and it only takes about 25 minutes to cook. A crisp green salad with a tart vinaigrette completes the meal nicely.

2 ounces goat cheese

1 teaspoon dried basil

1 teaspoon dried oregano

4 boneless, skinless chicken breast halves

¾ teaspoon salt

½ teaspoon freshly ground black pepper

4 slices prosciutto

2 tablespoons olive oil

1. Preheat the oven to 375°F.

2. In a small bowl, stir together the goat cheese, basil, and oregano.

3. Place the chicken breasts between sheets of plastic wrap or waxed paper, and pound them to about ¼-inch to ½-inch thick.

4. Divide the goat cheese mixture evenly among the 4 portions of chicken, spreading it in a strip down the middle. Roll the chicken breasts up around the cheese and season them all over with the salt and pepper. Wrap each chicken roll in a piece of prosciutto, and use toothpicks to secure. ▶

5. Heat the olive oil in an oven-safe skillet over medium-high heat. When the oil is very hot, add the chicken and cook, turning occasionally, for 6 to 8 minutes, until the chicken is browned on all sides. Transfer the skillet to the oven and bake for about 15 minutes, until the chicken is cooked through.

6. Remove from the oven and let rest for about 5 minutes. Slice each roll into several pieces, place on plates, and serve immediately.

Chicken in Enchilada Sauce

SERVES 4   PREP TIME: 5 MINUTES   COOK TIME: 25 MINUTES

● ● ● *A deliciously rich tomato-based sauce seasoned with chili powder is what makes a great enchilada. This sauce easily measures up—you won't even miss the tortillas. A drizzle of Cashew Cheese provides the ultimate finishing touch, or if you are on the yellow or green plan, you can substitute a few ounces of grated sharp Cheddar or Monterey Jack cheese.*

2 tablespoons coconut oil

1 medium onion, finely diced

1 (16-ounce) can tomato purée

4 garlic cloves, minced

2 tablespoons chili powder

½ teaspoon ground cumin

½ teaspoon dried oregano

½ teaspoon salt

1 pound cooked, shredded chicken

1 medium avocado, sliced, for garnish

¼ cup chopped cilantro, for garnish

1 lime, cut into 4 wedges, for garnish

½ cup Cashew Cheese (page 373), for garnish (optional)

1. Preheat the oven to 375°F.

2. Heat the coconut oil in a large skillet over medium-high heat. Add the onion and cook, stirring frequently, for about 5 minutes, until softened. Stir in the tomato purée, garlic, chili powder, cumin, oregano, and salt, and bring to a boil. Reduce the heat to medium-low, and simmer, stirring occasionally, for 15 minutes.

3. Using an immersion blender or a food processor or blender (in batches), purée the sauce until smooth. ▶

4. Place the chicken in a 9-by-13-inch baking dish and pour the sauce over the top. Cover tightly with foil, and bake for 10 minutes, until hot and bubbling.

5. Serve immediately, garnished with avocado slices, cilantro, lime wedges, and Cashew Cheese, if using.

TIP   Any simply prepared leftover chicken will do, such as a roasted chicken. If you don't have any chicken left over, pick up a rotisserie chicken at a local market, and you'll be able to turn it into a couple of quick, satisfying meals.

Rosemary Chicken
with Vegetables

SERVES 6   PREP TIME: 5 MINUTES   COOK TIME: I HOUR

● ● ●   *Pieces of dark-meat chicken baked alongside cauliflower, carrots, and zucchini make this delicious one-dish dinner an easy meal. Just toss the ingredients together in a baking dish and roast to perfection. For variety, add other root vegetables to the pan like turnips, parsnips, or celery root.*

2 pounds bone-in chicken drumsticks and thighs
Salt
Freshly ground black pepper
2 cups cauliflower florets
1 cup halved baby carrots
1 onion, quartered
1 zucchini, cut into 1-inch chunks
2 tablespoons dried rosemary
¼ cup gluten-free chicken broth

1. Preheat the oven to 400°F.

2. Season the chicken with salt and pepper and set aside.

3. Put the cauliflower, carrots, onion, and zucchini in a 9-by-13-inch glass baking dish, and top with the chicken.

4. Sprinkle the chicken and vegetables with the rosemary, and drizzle with the chicken broth.

5. Roast for 45 to 55 minutes, or until the chicken is cooked through and very tender. Let the chicken rest for 5 minutes before serving.

6. Serve the chicken hot with the vegetables alongside.

Pan-Seared Chicken Veracruz

SERVES 4   PREP TIME: 10 MINUTES   COOK TIME: 20 MINUTES

This simple chicken dish from the Mexican state of Veracruz melds the cuisines of Mexico and Spain. It's a deliciously spicy mix of Latin American and European flavors, featuring tomatoes, garlic, chiles, and olives.

1 tablespoon olive oil

4 skin-on, bone-in chicken breast halves (about 1½ pounds total)

1 teaspoon dried oregano

1 teaspoon salt

3 medium tomatoes, diced

2 medium zucchini, thinly sliced

1 medium onion, halved and thinly sliced

2 jalapeño chile peppers, seeded and very thinly sliced

4 garlic cloves, minced

¼ cup thinly sliced black olives

1 cup dry white wine

1. Preheat the oven to 350°F.

2. Heat the olive oil in a large skillet over medium-high heat. Sprinkle the chicken with the oregano and ½ teaspoon of salt, and place them in the skillet. Cook, turning once or twice, for about 10 minutes, until they are browned on all sides.

3. Transfer the chicken pieces to a baking dish. Scatter the tomatoes, zucchini, onion, chiles, garlic, and olives over the chicken. Sprinkle the remaining ½ teaspoon of salt and the wine over the top. Bake the chicken for 20 to 25 minutes, until the vegetables are soft and the chicken is cooked through.

4. Serve the chicken hot, topped with some of the vegetables.

Creamy Green Chile Chicken

SERVES 4   PREP TIME: 5 MINUTES   COOK TIME: 25 MINUTES

● ● ●   *Almonds and almond milk give this simple chicken dish a rich, creamy flavor that is out of this world. Using fresh green chiles rather than the usual canned variety gives it extra homemade goodness.*

2 cups unsweetened almond milk

½ cup chicken broth

¾ cup chopped seeded fresh New Mexico green chiles

3 scallions, sliced, white and green parts separated

3 tablespoons slivered almonds, toasted

1 garlic clove, thinly sliced

½ teaspoon salt, plus ¼ teaspoon

1 tablespoon olive oil

1½ pounds chicken breast tenders

1 tablespoon sesame seeds, toasted

1. In a medium saucepan, add the almond milk, chicken broth, green chiles, white parts of the scallions, almonds, garlic, and ¼ teaspoon of the salt, and bring to a boil. Lower the heat and simmer the mixture for about 20 minutes, until reduced by half. Using an immersion blender or a blender, purée the reduced mixture.

2. While the sauce is cooking, heat the olive oil in a large, nonstick skillet over medium-high heat. Sprinkle the remaining ½ teaspoon salt on the chicken, and add the chicken to the skillet. Cook for about 2 minutes, until browned on the bottom, then flip over and cook for about 2 minutes, until browned on the other side.

3. Transfer the puréed sauce to the skillet with the chicken, and bring to a simmer. Reduce the heat to medium, and cook for 5 minutes, until the chicken is thoroughly cooked. Serve the chicken hot, garnished with the reserved green parts of the scallions and the sesame seeds.

TIP   Use chicken breast tenders to cut down on prep time. If you can't find them, or you already have whole chicken breasts, you can always cut them into filets or cutlets yourself. Just cut the chicken breast off the bone, and cut each breast into 3 or 4 strips. Lay the strips between pieces of plastic wrap and pound to about ¼ inch thick. Then follow the recipe.

Chicken Pad Thai with Yellow Squash Noodles

SERVES 4   PREP TIME: 10 MINUTES   COOK TIME: 15 MINUTES

● ● ●   *Reproducing all the crave-worthy flavor of traditional Pad Thai, this version substitutes ribbons of yellow squash for the usual rice noodles. It also calls for macadamia nuts in place of peanuts, but you may substitute any nut you prefer, such as almonds, hazelnuts, or even pine nuts.*

4 medium yellow squash

¼ cup almond butter

½ cup coconut aminos

¼ teaspoon fish sauce

Juice of 1 lime, divided

1 teaspoon salt

¼ teaspoon cayenne pepper

1 tablespoon sesame oil

1 pound diced chicken breast

1 shallot, minced

3 garlic cloves, minced

⅓ cup chopped macadamia nuts

2 tablespoons chopped cilantro, for garnish

1. To make the squash noodles, lay a box grater on its side, placing the side with the large holes on top. Grate the squash lengthwise in long strokes to cut long, thin, noodle-shaped ribbons.

2. Fill a pot fitted with a steamer basket with 1 inch of water, and bring to a boil. Place the squash ribbons in the steamer basket, and cover and steam for about 5 minutes, until just tender.

3. In a small bowl, mix the almond butter, coconut aminos, fish sauce, half the lime juice, salt, and cayenne pepper.

4. Heat the sesame oil in a large skillet over high heat. Add the chicken and cook, stirring frequently, for about 5 minutes, until cooked through. Add the shallot and garlic and cook, stirring, for 1 minute. Add the nuts, reserving 1 tablespoon for garnish, and continue to cook, stirring, for 2 minutes more. Add the almond butter mixture, and toss to coat well.

5. Reduce the heat to low and add in the squash noodles. Stir them in gently. Cook just until heated through, about 2 minutes. Serve immediately, garnished with cilantro, the reserved 1 tablespoon chopped nuts, and of the remaining lime juice.

Roasted Whole Chicken
with Fresh Herbs

SERVES 4 TO 6   PREP TIME: 10 MINUTES   COOK TIME: 1½ HOURS

● ● ● *Though this recipe may take a while to cook, the preparation could not be simpler. It's a fantastic recipe for feeding a crowd. Freeze the chicken giblets and carcass to make homemade chicken stock.*

1 (3-pound) roasting chicken
Salt
Freshly ground black pepper
1 tablespoon chopped fresh thyme, plus a few whole sprigs
1 tablespoon chopped fresh rosemary, plus a few whole sprigs
1 teaspoon minced garlic, plus 2 whole heads
2 lemons, halved

1. Preheat the oven to 425°F.

2. Remove the giblets bag from the cavity of the chicken, and rinse the chicken inside and out with cold water. Pat dry with paper towels.

3. Place the chicken in a roasting pan, and season liberally with salt and pepper. Sprinkle with the chopped thyme, rosemary, and minced garlic, and rub in to the skin. Tie the legs together with string, and tuck the wings under the body. Scatter the garlic heads, halved lemons, and herb sprigs over and around the chicken.

4. Roast for 60 to 70 minutes, until the chicken's thigh juices run clear when pierced with the point of a sharp knife.

5. Remove to a cutting board, and let it sit for 10 minutes before carving.

TIP   If your oven is large enough, save time by roasting two chickens at once. Eat one for supper tonight and save the other to use in sandwiches, salads, and casseroles throughout the week.

Roasted Chicken Breasts with Mustard and Greens

SERVES 4   PREP TIME: 5 MINUTES   COOK TIME: I HOUR

● ● ●   *The beauty of a roasted chicken dish is that with just a little prep, you can stick it in the oven, and forget about it until it's time to eat. Simply give bone-in, skin-on chicken breasts a blanketing of zesty Dijon mustard and a sprinkle of smoky paprika before slipping them into a hot oven. Just before the chicken is finished roasting, give the garlic-spiked greens a quick sauté and—voilà!—dinner is ready.*

4 bone-in, skin-on chicken breast halves
¼ cup Dijon mustard
1 teaspoon smoked paprika
½ teaspoon salt
½ teaspoon freshly ground black pepper
2 tablespoons olive oil
1 pound Swiss chard, tough center ribs removed,
   leaves julienned
2 garlic cloves, minced

1. Preheat the oven to 375°F.

2. Arrange the chicken pieces in a single layer in a large baking dish, and spread the mustard evenly over the chicken. Sprinkle with the paprika, salt, and pepper. Bake the chicken in the preheated oven for 45 to 55 minutes, until it is cooked through.

3. Meanwhile, heat the olive oil in a large saucepan set over medium-high heat. Add the chard and garlic, cover, and cook for about 2 minutes, until the greens are mostly wilted. Uncover and continue cooking, stirring frequently, until the greens are completely wilted. Remove from the heat.

4. Serve the hot chicken on top of the greens.

> TIP   Swiss chard is widely available and comes with stems in a variety of pretty colors, but you can substitute other hearty greens, such as kale, for the chard in this recipe. Mustard greens, would complement the dish especially well, adding a lovely additional dose of mustard flavor.

Spice-Rubbed Grilled Turkey Legs

SERVES 4   PREP TIME: 5 MINUTES   COOK TIME: I HOUR IO MINUTES

● ● ●   *At Thanksgiving dinner at our house, everyone wants a leg—after all, the legs are loaded with the most succulent dark meat—but even the biggest turkey only delivers two. So why not forget the rest of the turkey, and just buy a bunch of legs? Here they are coated with a flavorful mixture of spices and grilled to perfection.*

- 2 tablespoons ground cumin
- 2 tablespoons garlic powder
- 2 teaspoons freshly ground black pepper
- 1 teaspoon salt
- 1 teaspoon cayenne pepper
- 4 turkey legs
- Coconut oil for basting

1. Preheat the grill to medium-high heat.

2. In a small bowl, combine the cumin, garlic powder, black pepper, salt, and cayenne pepper and stir to mix.

3. Rub the spice mixture all over the drumsticks.

4. Cook the drumsticks on the hottest part of the grill for 10 to 12 minutes, turning every 3 to 4 minutes to sear all sides.

5. Move the drumsticks away from the high heat (you can either slide coals over to create an indirect heat zone, or turn off one burner of a gas grill to create a cooler cooking zone), and cook for 60 minutes, turning every 10 minutes, until the drumsticks are cooked through. Baste the drumsticks occasionally with coconut oil during the last 20 minutes of cooking.

6. Serve immediately.

Chipotle Turkey Burgers

SERVES 4   PREP TIME: 5 MINUTES   COOK TIME: 15 MINUTES

Ground turkey is a lean alternative to ground beef, and it makes a flavorful burger. These delicious chipotle turkey burgers are a tasty example of just how appetizing ground turkey can be. Serve them topped with lettuce, tomato, and onion slices. Add Pico de Gallo (page 363) and Chipotle Guacamole (page 162) for Mexican flair or go the more traditional burger route with pickle slices, mustard, and Sugar-Free Ketchup (page 366).

1 pound ground turkey

2 tablespoons minced red onion

1 tablespoon almond flour

1 garlic clove, minced

1 teaspoon chipotle chile powder

4 large lettuce leaves, for serving

1. Preheat the broiler to high.

2. In a medium bowl, add the turkey, onion, almond flour, garlic, and chile powder, and mix well by hand.

3. Shape the mixture into 4 patties, and place them on a broiler pan.

4. Broil the turkey burgers for 4 to 6 minutes on each side, until cooked through.

5. Serve hot, wrapped in lettuce leaves, with your favorite toppings.

TIP   Uncooked turkey burgers freeze well. Mix up a double or triple batch of this recipe, wrap the extra patties individually in plastic wrap, and freeze for quick future meals. Defrost overnight or all day in the refrigerator before needed.

Quick Turkey Chili

SERVES 4   PREP TIME: IO MINUTES   COOK TIME: 20 MINUTES

● ● ●   *This quick and flavorful turkey chili is a perfect dish to serve on a weeknight when you've limited time to get a healthy dinner on the table. Serve it topped with a dollop of Chipotle Guacamole (page 162) if you like.*

2 tablespoons olive oil

1 onion, diced

2 garlic cloves, minced

1 green bell pepper, diced

1 pound ground turkey

2 teaspoons chili powder

1 teaspoon ground cumin

¼ teaspoon ground cinnamon

1 teaspoon dried oregano

1 teaspoon salt

½ teaspoon freshly ground black pepper

1 (15-ounce) can diced tomatoes, drained

1 (15-ounce) can black beans, drained and rinsed

1 (4½-ounce) can diced green chiles

1. Heat the olive oil in a large skillet over medium-high heat. Add the onion, garlic, and bell pepper and cook, stirring frequently, for about 5 minutes, until the onion is softened. Transfer the vegetables to a bowl.

2. In the same skillet, add the turkey over medium heat and brown, cooking for about 5 minutes, stirring frequently. Stir in the chili powder, cumin, cinnamon, oregano, salt, and pepper. Add the tomatoes, black beans, and green chiles, and stir to combine. Return the onion mixture to the skillet, and cook, stirring occasionally, for about 5 minutes, until the chili is hot and bubbly.

3. Serve immediately.

Turkey Meatloaf with Creole Seasoning

SERVES 4 TO 6 PREP TIME: 5 MINUTES COOK TIME: 45 MINUTES

● ◉ ● *This simple turkey meatloaf is flavored with Creole seasoning mix and bathed in a spicy mixture of Sugar-Free Ketchup and hot pepper sauce. It makes a tasty dinner served with a side salad or Mashed Parsnips with Garlic (page 202)—then, the following day, simply wrap leftovers in lettuce leaves for a satisfying lunch. You can find Creole seasoning mix in the spice aisle of the supermarket.*

1½ pounds ground turkey

1 onion, diced

½ red or green bell pepper, diced

2 celery stalks, diced

1 egg, lightly beaten

½ cup Sugar-Free Ketchup, divided (page 366)

2 garlic cloves, minced

1 tablespoon Creole seasoning mix

1 teaspoon salt

½ teaspoon freshly ground black pepper

1 tablespoon hot pepper sauce

1. Preheat the oven to 375°F. Line a rimmed baking sheet with parchment paper.

2. In a large bowl, mix together the turkey, onion, bell pepper, celery, egg, ¼ cup of ketchup, garlic, Creole seasoning mix, salt, and pepper. Mix to combine.

3. Transfer the mixture to the prepared baking sheet and form it into a loaf shape.

4. In a small bowl, stir together the remaining ¼ cup ketchup and the hot pepper sauce. Spoon the ketchup mixture over the meatloaf, and spread it out evenly with the back of the spoon.

5. Bake for about 45 minutes, until the meatloaf is cooked through and is nicely browned on top.

6. Let the meatloaf rest for 5 minutes before slicing. Serve hot.

Turkey Meatballs with Zucchini Spaghetti and Spicy Tomato Sauce

SERVES 4   PREP TIME: I5 MINUTES   COOK TIME: 20 MINUTES

● ● ●   *Light ground turkey spiked with Fresh Basil Pesto makes for delicious meatballs. Served over ribbons of zucchini in Spicy Tomato Sauce, these meatballs are genuine old-fashioned comfort food. This dish is lighter and far more nutritious than the original, yet still undeniably delicious.*

- 2 tablespoons olive oil, plus 1 tablespoon, plus more for the parchment paper
- ¾ pound ground turkey
- 2 tablespoons Fresh Basil Pesto (page 365)
- ½ teaspoon salt
- ½ teaspoon freshly ground black pepper
- 2 cups Spicy Tomato Sauce (page 368)
- 2 large zucchini, trimmed

1. Preheat the oven to 375°F. Line a large rimmed baking sheet with lightly oiled parchment paper.

2. In a medium bowl, add the turkey, Fresh Basil Pesto, salt, and pepper, and mix well. Wet your hands and form the mixture into 1½-inch balls. As you form the balls, place them on the prepared baking sheet with a bit of space between them. Brush 2 tablespoons olive oil lightly over the tops of the meatballs, and bake for about 15 minutes, until they are lightly browned on the outside and cooked through.

3. Meanwhile, heat the Spicy Tomato Sauce in a large skillet over medium heat, letting it simmer.

4. When the meatballs are done, add them to the simmering sauce, and cook until the rest of the meal is ready.

5. To make the zucchini spaghetti, lay a box grater on its side with the large holes on top. Grate the squash lengthwise in long strokes to cut long, thin, vaguely spaghetti-shaped ribbons.

6. Heat the remaining 1 tablespoon of olive oil in a large skillet over medium-high heat. Add the zucchini ribbons and cook, stirring frequently, until just tender, for about 3 minutes.

7. Serve the zucchini noodles topped with sauce and a few meatballs.

> TIP   If you don't have some of the Fresh Basil Pesto recipe on hand for these meatballs, you can substitute either a store-bought pesto (just be sure to check the ingredients for additives) or you can use 2 tablespoons minced fresh basil and 2 minced garlic cloves in place of the pesto.

Oven-Roasted Duck Breast with Wild Mushrooms

SERVES 4
PREP TIME: 5 MINUTES (PLUS I HOUR TO MARINATE THE MEAT)
COOK TIME: 40 MINUTES

Duck breast is often overlooked by home cooks, but it's really a cinch to prepare, resulting in a rich, elegant dish that is sure to impress guests. Here star anise contributes an exotic flavor to a simple seared and oven-roasted duck breast on a bed of succulent mushrooms.

- 2 (8-ounce) boneless duck breasts, skin-on
- 1 whole star anise pod
- ½ teaspoon whole black peppercorns
- 1 teaspoon salt, plus ½ teaspoon
- ½ cup chicken broth
- 2 tablespoons olive oil
- 10 ounces porcini or other mushrooms, thinly sliced
- 2 small leeks, white and light green parts halved lengthwise, thinly sliced, and rinsed

1. Using a very sharp knife, score the skin of the duck breasts in a crisscross pattern.

2. In a spice grinder or using a mortar and pestle, grind the star anise, peppercorns, and 1 teaspoon of the salt together.

3. Rub the spice mixture all over the duck breasts. Place the duck in a bowl, and pour the broth over the top. Refrigerate for at least 1 hour or as long as overnight.

4. Preheat the oven to 400°F. ▶

5. Heat the oil in a large, heavy skillet over medium-high heat. Add the mushrooms and leeks along with the remaining ½ teaspoon of salt, and cook, stirring frequently, for about 10 minutes until the mushrooms have softened.

6. Meanwhile, heat a heavy, oven-safe skillet over medium-high heat. Add the duck breast, skin-side down, and cook for about 6 minutes, until the skin is nicely browned. Flip the duck breasts over, and place the skillet in the oven to roast for 6 to 8 minutes for medium-rare.

7. Let the duck rest in the pan for about 5 minutes, then remove to a cutting board. Slice thinly and serve hot with the cooked leeks and mushrooms spooned over the top.

Garlicky Lemon Chicken
with Fresh Thyme

SERVES 4
PREP TIME: 10 MINUTES (PLUS 2 OR MORE HOURS FOR MARINATING)
COOK TIME: 70 MINUTES

Marinated in lemon juice and zest, and spiked with lots of fresh garlic and thyme, this simple chicken dish contains only a few ingredients but is infused with intense flavor. And roasting the chicken pieces in the oven at high heat turns the skin a crispy golden brown.

Zest and juice of 3 lemons
6 garlic cloves, minced
1 tablespoon minced fresh thyme, plus 6 sprigs
1 teaspoon salt
½ teaspoon freshly ground black pepper
1½ pounds bone-in, skin-on chicken legs and thighs
¼ cup coconut oil

1. In a small bowl, add the lemon zest, lemon juice, garlic, minced thyme, salt, and pepper, and whisk together to combine.

2. Place the chicken in a large bowl or resealable plastic bag. Pour the marinade over the chicken, toss to coat, and refrigerate for 2 hours (or as long as overnight).

3. To cook the chicken, preheat the oven to 400°F.

4. Arrange the chicken skin-side up in a single layer in a roasting pan or baking dish. Pour the marinade over the top, scatter the thyme sprigs on the chicken, and drizzle with the coconut oil.

5. Bake for 60 to 70 minutes, until the skin is nicely browned and the chicken is cooked through. Serve immediately.

Chiles Rellenos Stuffed with Duck

SERVES 4   PREP TIME: I5 MINUTES   COOK TIME: 35 MINUTES

● ● ●   *Gone are the heavily battered cheese-laden chiles rellenos of days past. These contain a rich duck-and-olive filling, making them far more sophisticated in flavor. If you have leftover roast duck meat, or if you can buy prepared duck confit, substitute it for the duck legs here, to save a bit of time and effort.*

> 2 (8-ounce) duck leg quarters (thighs and drumsticks),
>   skin removed
> 4 medium poblano chile peppers or New Mexico green chiles
> 1 teaspoon olive oil
> ½ medium onion, diced
> 1 garlic clove, minced
> 1 large tomato, diced
> 1 tablespoon white vinegar
> ⅓ cup chopped pitted green olives
> ¼ cup slivered almonds, chopped
> ¼ teaspoon salt

1. Preheat a grill or grill pan to medium.

2. Place the duck and chiles on the grill. Cook, turning occasionally, for about 15 minutes. The duck should be cooked through and the chiles blistered on all sides. Remove to a plate and let cool until cool enough to handle.

3. Strip the duck meat from the bones, and chop it finely. Carefully slide the blistered skins off of the chiles. Make a slit down the center of each chile, leaving the stem intact, and remove the seeds.

4. Preheat the oven to 375°F.

5. Heat the olive oil in a large skillet over medium heat. Add the onion and garlic and cook for about 5 minutes, stirring frequently, until they begin to soften. Stir in the tomato and vinegar and cook, stirring frequently, for about 3 minutes, until the tomato starts to break down. Add the duck meat, olives, almonds, and salt, stir to mix well, and remove from the heat.

6. Fill each chile with about ½ cup of the duck mixture, and place them, seam-side up, on a large, rimmed baking sheet. Bake for about 15 minutes, until heated through. Serve hot.

THIRTEEN

MEAT

Pork and Cilantro Meatballs

SERVES 6   PREP TIME: 15 MINUTES   COOK TIME: 25 MINUTES

Preparing these simple meatballs is a snap, and you'll find that baking them in the oven rather than frying them in a skillet cuts down dramatically on their hands-on prep time. Serve them with zucchini noodles or steamed or stir-fried vegetables. Or stuff them into lettuce leaves for an Asian-style, grain-free "meatball sandwich."

2 tablespoons olive oil, plus more for the parchment paper
2 pounds ground pork
½ onion, chopped fine
1 teaspoon salt
1 teaspoon coconut aminos
2 cups (packed) chopped baby spinach
½ cup chopped fresh cilantro
¼ cup diced water chestnuts
2 eggs, lightly beaten

1. Preheat the oven to 400°F. Line a large rimmed baking sheet with parchment paper brushed with olive oil.

2. In a large bowl, add the pork, onion, salt, coconut aminos, spinach, cilantro, water chestnuts, and eggs, and mix together with your hands. Form the mixture into 1½-inch balls, and arrange them on the prepared baking sheet.

3. Brush the tops of the meatballs with the remaining 2 tablespoons olive oil. Bake the meatballs for about 25 minutes, until beginning to brown on the outside and cooked through.

4. Serve immediately, or store in the refrigerator for up to 3 days or in the freezer for up to 3 months.

Pork Chops Stuffed with Spinach and Capers

SERVES 4   PREP TIME: 10 MINUTES   COOK TIME: 25 MINUTES

● ● ● *Stuffing a pork chop turns it into an impressive presentation worthy of guests. It also adds both flavor and moisture to the meat. Here a moist spinach stuffing is flavored with sun-dried tomatoes and bacon, creating a finished dish that's easy to make but elegant enough for your next dinner party.*

3 slices bacon

2 garlic cloves, minced

6 sun-dried tomatoes, drained and diced

1 (10-ounce) box frozen spinach, thawed and excess water squeezed out

½ teaspoon salt, plus more for seasoning chops

½ teaspoon black pepper, plus more for seasoning chops

¼ teaspoon dried thyme

4 (4- to 6-ounce) center-cut pork chops

1½ cups chicken broth

Zest of ½ lemon

2 tablespoons freshly squeezed lemon juice

2 teaspoons Dijon mustard

1 tablespoon coconut oil

1 tablespoon capers

1. Heat a medium skillet over medium-high heat and add the bacon. Cook for about 4 minutes per side, until browned and crisp. Drain on paper towels and crumble.

2. Reduce the heat to medium, and add the garlic to the bacon fat in the pan. Cook, stirring, for 1 minute. Add the sun-dried tomatoes, spinach, salt, pepper, and thyme and cook, stirring frequently, for 2 minutes. Transfer the mixture to a medium bowl, and add the crumbled bacon. ▶

3. To prepare the pork chops, lay them flat on the work surface and, using a very sharp knife, cut a horizontal pocket into the thickest part of each. Fill each pocket with the spinach and sun-dried tomato mixture, dividing the mixture equally among the 4 chops. Secure with toothpicks if needed. Season the pork chops on both sides with salt and pepper.

4. Stir together the chicken broth, lemon zest, lemon juice, and mustard in a small bowl.

5. Using the same skillet, heat the coconut oil over medium-high heat. Add the pork chops and cook for about 4 minutes per side, until golden brown and cooked through. Remove the chops to a plate, tent with aluminum foil, and let rest for 5 minutes.

6. Meanwhile, in the skillet over medium-high heat, add the chicken broth mixture, and cook for about 8 minutes, stirring and scraping up any flavorful browned bits from the bottom of the pan. Continue cooking and stirring for about 5 minutes, until the liquid is reduced by about half. Add the capers and cook for 1 minute.

7. Serve the pork chops hot with the sauce spooned over the top.

Coffee and Chipotle–Rubbed Oven-Roasted Pork Chops

SERVES 4
PREP TIME: 5 MINUTES (PLUS OVERNIGHT FOR MARINATING)
COOK TIME: 15 MINUTES

● ● ●   *Coffee and spices lend intriguing flavor to these juicy pork chops. Serve them on a bed of puréed cauliflower or parsnips with garlicky sautéed greens alongside. You'll likely have extra spice rub left over, so store it in a jar for another use—it would be equally delicious on steak or chicken.*

1 tablespoon salt
1 tablespoon finely ground coffee beans
   (French or espresso roast)
½ tablespoon freshly ground black pepper
½ teaspoon ground chipotle chile pepper
½ teaspoon garlic powder
½ teaspoon cinnamon
½ teaspoon cumin
½ teaspoon ground allspice
4 thick-cut, bone-in loin pork chops
2½ tablespoons coconut oil

1. In a small bowl, stir together the salt, coffee, black pepper, chipotle chile pepper, garlic powder, cinnamon, cumin, and allspice.

2. Rub the spice mixture all over both sides of the pork chops. Cover and refrigerate the pork chops overnight or all day.

3. Before cooking, bring the pork chops to room temperature by setting them on the countertop for 30 minutes.

4. Preheat the oven to 350°F. ▶

5. Heat the coconut oil a large, oven-safe skillet over medium-high heat. When the oil is very hot, add the pork chops, and cook for 2 to 3 minutes per side, until nicely browned.

6. Transfer the pan to the oven, and cook for about 10 minutes, until the meat is cooked through.

7. Remove the pork chops to a platter, and let rest for 10 minutes before serving hot.

Stir-Fried Pork with Cabbage and Cashews

SERVES 4 PREP TIME: 10 MINUTES COOK TIME: 10 MINUTES

● ● ● *A quick stir-fry creates a healthy meal you can bring to the table in a hurry. For a bit of extra spice, add 1 to 2 teaspoons of chili paste to the sauce.*

¼ cup coconut aminos

¼ cup rice vinegar

¼ cup Chinese rice wine

¼ cup cashew butter

1 tablespoon chopped peeled fresh ginger, plus 1 tablespoon

1 garlic clove, finely chopped

½ teaspoon Chinese five-spice powder

2 tablespoons coconut oil, plus 1 tablespoon

1 pound pork tenderloin, trimmed and sliced into strips

6 cups sliced Napa cabbage

½ cup unsalted cashews

½ cup chopped scallions, for garnish

1. In a small bowl, add the coconut aminos, vinegar, rice wine, cashew butter, 1 tablespoon of the ginger, garlic, and five-spice powder, and whisk to mix. Set the sauce aside.

2. Heat 2 tablespoons of coconut oil in a large skillet over medium-high heat. Add the pork strips in a single layer, and cook for about 2 minutes, until the pork begins to brown on the bottom. Continue to cook, stirring, for 2 to 3 minutes, until cooked through. Transfer the meat to a plate.

3. Heat the remaining 1 tablespoon coconut oil in the pan. Add the remaining 1 tablespoon ginger, cabbage, and cashews and cook, stirring, for 2 minutes. Return the pork to the pan and add the sauce. Bring to a boil and cook, stirring frequently, for 2 minutes. Serve hot, garnished with the scallions.

Roasted Pork Loin with Oregano and Garlic

SERVES 8   PREP TIME: 5 MINUTES   COOK TIME: 55 MINUTES

A pork loin only takes a few minutes to prepare before you put it in the oven, but it can feed a large number of people— a 2½-pound roast, for example, can serve as many as eight people. For a hearty Sunday supper, complete the meal with Mashed Parsnips with Garlic (page 202), roasted carrots, or other root vegetables.

1 (2½-pound) boneless pork loin

1½ teaspoons salt

½ teaspoon freshly ground black pepper

1 tablespoon minced garlic

2 teaspoons dried oregano

1. Preheat the oven to 400°F. Line a roasting pan with aluminum foil.

2. Trim the fat from the pork, if desired, leaving a thin layer of fat on top. Season with the salt and pepper.

3. Rub the garlic into the pork, and sprinkle with the oregano. Place the roast fat-side down in the roasting pan.

4. Roast for 30 minutes, then turn the pork over. Roast for 25 minutes, or until it reaches an internal temperature of 155°F on an instrant-read meat thermometer.

5. Remove the roast to a cutting board, and let it rest 10 minutes before slicing. Slice into ¼-inch-thick slices and serve immediately.

Pork Stew with Fennel and Herbs

SERVES 6 TO 8   PREP TIME: IO MINUTES   COOK TIME: 3 HOURS

● ● ● *Fennel adds an exotic flavor to this rustic stew, which makes a lovely family supper. This recipe produces a lot, but the leftovers are even more flavorful than the original, so plan to eat this stew for more than one meal throughout the coming week. The dish also freezes well.*

2½ pounds pork shoulder, trimmed and cut into 2-inch chunks
¾ teaspoon salt, plus ¾ teaspoon
¾ teaspoon freshly ground black pepper, plus ¾ teaspoon
1 tablespoon olive oil, plus 1 tablespoon, plus 1 tablespoon
1 medium onion, halved and thinly sliced
¾ cup chicken broth
8 cups thinly sliced fennel (2 to 3 medium bulbs), plus ¼ cup chopped fronds, for garnish
4 garlic cloves, minced
1 tablespoon finely chopped fresh rosemary
2 teaspoons finely chopped fresh oregano
1 (28-ounce) can whole tomatoes, drained

1. Season the pork chunks with ¾ teaspoon of the salt and ¾ teaspoon of the pepper.

2. Heat 1 tablespoon of the olive oil in a large stockpot or Dutch oven over medium-high heat. Add about one-half the pork and cook, stirring, for about 5 minutes, until browned on all sides. Remove the browned pork to a medium bowl. Add an additional 1 tablespoon olive oil and repeat with the remaining pork.

3. In the same pot, heat the remaining tablespoon of oil. Add the onion and cook, stirring, for about 5 minutes, until softened. Add the chicken broth to the pan, bring to a boil, and deglaze the pan by scraping up any flavorful browned bits on the bottom. Return the pork to the pot, and add the fennel, garlic, rosemary, oregano, and the remaining ¾ teaspoon each of the salt and pepper.

4. Add the tomatoes, increase the heat to high, and bring to a boil. Reduce the heat to low, and cover and cook for 2 to 3 hours, stirring occasionally, until the meat is very tender. Add 1 or 2 tablespoons water if the mixture seems dry.

5. Serve hot, garnished with the reserved fennel fronds.

Vietnamese Stir-Fried Pork

SERVES 4

PREP TIME: 10 MINUTES (PLUS 15 MINUTES TO MARINATE)

COOK TIME: 10 MINUTES

This dish is a quick stir-fry flavored with fish sauce, chiles, garlic, and ginger. Serve it with steamed carrots or sautéed cabbage for a simple meal that's at once healthy and satisfying.

2 tablespoons finely chopped peeled fresh ginger

2 serrano or jalapeño chiles, seeded and diced

4 garlic cloves, finely chopped

2 tablespoons fish sauce, plus 1 tablespoon

1 tablespoon freshly squeezed lime juice, plus 1 tablespoon

½ teaspoon freshly ground black pepper

1 pound pork tenderloin, trimmed and sliced ¼ inch thick

1 teaspoon olive oil or coconut oil, plus 2 teaspoons

2 onions, thinly sliced

¼ cup sliced fresh cilantro

1. In a large bowl, add the ginger, chiles, garlic, 1 tablespoon fish sauce, 1 tablespoon lime juice, and pepper, and stir to combine. Add the pork slices and stir to coat well. Marinate at room temperature for 15 minutes.

2. In a small bowl, add the remaining 2 tablespoons fish sauce and 1 tablespoon lime juice, and whisk to combine.

3. Heat 1 teaspoon of the olive oil in a large skillet over medium-high heat. Add the onions and cook, stirring frequently, for about 5 minutes, until softened. Remove the onions to a plate. Add the remaining 2 teaspoons olive oil to the pan, and raise the heat to high. Add the pork and cook, stirring, for about 3 minutes, until browned and just cooked through. Add the fish sauce and lime juice mixture, and return the onions to the pan. Cook, stirring frequently, until the mixture is heated through. Serve immediately, garnished with cilantro.

TIP   To make slicing the pork easier, first wrap the uncooked tenderloin in plastic wrap and chill in the freezer for about 30 minutes.

Quick-and-Easy Pork Chops with Sautéed Mushrooms

SERVES 4   PREP TIME: 5 MINUTES   COOK TIME: 25 MINUTES

● ● ● *Here a simple-to-prepare mushroom sauce dresses up plain pork chops in no time. If you're craving a "meat and potatoes" style meal, these chops served with puréed cauliflower or Mashed Parsnips with Garlic (page 202) are sure to satisfy.*

4 bone-in, center-cut loin pork chops
1 teaspoon salt
½ teaspoon freshly ground black pepper
1 tablespoon coconut oil
1 onion, sliced
3 garlic cloves, minced
1 pound mushrooms (button or cremini, or a mixture), sliced
2 teaspoons minced fresh rosemary or ½ teaspoon
   dried rosemary
½ cup chicken broth

1. Season the pork chops with the salt and pepper. Heat the coconut oil in a large skillet over medium-high heat, and add the pork chops. Cook for about 3 minutes, until nicely browned on the bottom, then flip and cook for about 3 minutes, until the other side is nicely browned. Remove the chops to a plate.

2. Add the onion and garlic to the skillet, reduce the heat to medium, and cook, stirring frequently, for about 5 minutes, until softened. Add the mushrooms and rosemary and cook for 5 to 7 minutes, until the mushrooms are tender.

3. Add the chicken broth and bring to a simmer. Add the pork chops to the pan, cover, reduce the heat to medium-low, and simmer for about 8 minutes, until the pork is cooked through.

4. Serve the pork chops immediately, with the mushroom mixture spooned over the top.

Fajita Beef with Peppers

SERVES 4
PREP TIME: 10 MINUTES (PLUS AT LEAST 2 HOURS FOR MARINATING)
COOK TIME: 10 MINUTES

● ● ● *Fajitas are always a hit with young and old alike. These have all the flavor and color you expect from this Mexican favorite. The only element missing is the tortillas, but you won't even notice. Add your favorite fajita toppings like Chipotle Guacamole (page 162), sour cream, and Pico de Gallo (page 363), and set up a DIY fajita-wrap bar.*

- 2 tablespoons olive oil, plus 1 tablespoon, plus 1 tablespoon
- 3 tablespoons Worcestershire sauce
- ⅓ cup freshly squeezed lime juice
- 3 garlic cloves, minced
- 1 tablespoon ground cumin
- 1 tablespoon chili powder
- ½ teaspoon crushed red pepper flakes
- 1 teaspoon salt
- ½ teaspoon freshly ground black pepper
- 1½ pounds flank steak
- 1 large sweet onion, halved and thinly sliced
- 1 green bell pepper, seeded and sliced
- 1 orange bell pepper, seeded and sliced
- 1 red bell pepper, seeded and sliced
- 1 head large-leafed lettuce, for serving

1. In a large bowl, add 2 tablespoons of olive oil, the Worcestershire sauce, lime juice, garlic, cumin, chili powder, red pepper flakes, salt, and black pepper, and stir to combine.

2. Place the steak in a large, resealable plastic bag or baking dish, and add half of the marinade. Toss to coat. Place the vegetables in the large bowl with the remaining marinade, and toss to coat. Cover and refrigerate both the steak and the vegetables for at least 2 hours and as long as overnight. ▶

3. To cook, heat 1 tablespoon of the olive oil in a large skillet over medium-high heat. Add the vegetables and cook, stirring frequently, for about 5 minutes, until beginning to soften and charring a bit. Transfer the vegetables from the pan to a plate.

4. Add the remaining 1 tablespoon olive oil to the pan and heat over high heat. Add the meat and cook for about 2 minutes per side, until the meat is browned on the outside and medium rare.

5. Remove the meat to a cutting board and let rest for 5 minutes. Slice the meat across the grain into ¼-inch-thick slices, and serve hot with the vegetables, lettuce leaf wraps, and other toppings you like.

Beef Short Ribs Braised in Garlicky Tomato Sauce

SERVES 4 TO 6 **PREP TIME: 10 MINUTES** **COOK TIME: 3 HOURS 5 MINUTES**

Slow-cooked short ribs turn fall-off-the-bone tender after a couple of hours simmering in a rich tomato bath. Serve this dish with puréed cauliflower or Mashed Parsnips with Garlic (page 202) to soak up the luscious sauce.

2 tablespoons olive oil

5 pounds beef short ribs

1 teaspoon salt

½ teaspoon freshly ground black pepper

1 tablespoon dried basil

10 garlic cloves, smashed

2 (15-ounce) cans tomato sauce

3 tablespoons minced fresh parsley

1. Heat the olive oil in a large stockpot over medium-high heat.

2. Season the ribs with the salt and pepper, then add them to the pot. Cook for about 4 minutes, until browned on all sides.

3. Add the basil, garlic, and tomato sauce, and bring to a boil. Reduce the heat to low and simmer, covered, for about 2 hours, until the meat is very tender. Remove the lid from the pot and continue to simmer for 1 hour to reduce the sauce.

4. Serve hot, garnished with the parsley.

> **TIP** This dish can also be made in a slow cooker. After searing the ribs on the stove top, transfer them to the slow cooker, and add the remaining ingredients. Cook, covered, on low for 7 hours, remove the lid, and cook for 1 hour uncovered to reduce the sauce.

Bacon and Mushroom Burgers

SERVES 6   PREP TIME: I0 MINUTES   COOK TIME: I5 MINUTES

Bacon is the best thing to happen to burgers since, well, ever. Serve these lettuce-wrapped juicy burgers with Sugar-Free Ketchup (page 366), spicy mustard, sliced pickles, or any of your favorite toppings.

1 tablespoon olive oil, plus 1 tablespoon

½ pound cremini mushrooms, minced

1 pound ground beef

4 ounces bacon, minced

1½ teaspoons salt

½ teaspoon freshly ground black pepper

6 large lettuce leaves, like Bibb or butter lettuce

2 large tomatoes, sliced

1. Heat 1 tablespoon of the olive oil in a large skillet over medium heat. Add the mushrooms and cook for about 5 minutes, stirring frequently, until they've released their liquid and it has evaporated.

2. In a large bowl, mix the ground beef, bacon, sautéed mushrooms, salt, and pepper. Gently form the mixture into six ¾-inch-thick patties.

3. Heat the remaining 1 tablespoon olive oil in a large skillet over medium-high heat. Add the patties, and cook for about 3 minutes per side, until browned on the outside and medium rare (add 1 to 2 more minutes per side for well-done burgers). Drain the burgers on paper towels.

4. Serve the burgers hot, each on a lettuce leaf (for wrapping) and topped with tomato slices and any other toppings you choose.

> TIP   To keep burgers from shrinking into small patties with a mound in the middle, make an indentation with your thumb in the center of each after you form the patties.

Meaty Chili with Roasted Butternut Squash

SERVES 6 PREP TIME: 10 MINUTES COOK TIME: 3 HOURS

There's nothing quite as satisfying as a hearty bowl of spicy meaty chili. This one is topped with slightly sweet roasted butternut squash. Add any other chili-friendly toppings you like: diced avocado, diced red onions, sliced scallions, sour cream, shredded cheese, salsa, or chopped fresh cilantro.

1 pound peeled, cubed butternut squash

2 tablespoons olive oil, plus 1 tablespoon

½ teaspoon salt, plus 1 teaspoon

1 small onion, diced

¾ pound ground beef

½ pound ground lamb

2 tablespoons ground cumin

1 tablespoon smoked paprika

1 tablespoon chili powder

1 tablespoon garlic powder

½ teaspoon freshly ground black pepper

1 teaspoon cayenne pepper

⅛ teaspoon ground cloves

2 tablespoons tomato paste

1 cup beef broth

1 (14-ounce) can diced tomatoes with their juice

1. Preheat the oven to 350°F. Line a large, rimmed baking sheet with parchment paper.

2. Place the cubed squash on the prepared baking sheet, drizzle with 2 tablespoons of the olive oil, and sprinkle with ½ teaspoon of the salt. Roast the squash for about 45 minutes, until browned and tender. Remove from the oven and set aside.

3. Meanwhile, heat the remaining 1 tablespoon olive oil in a large stockpot over medium-high heat. Add the onion, beef, and lamb, and cook, stirring and breaking up the meat with a wooden spoon, for about 3 minutes, until browned. Add the cumin, paprika, chili powder, garlic powder, black pepper, cayenne pepper, cloves, and the remaining 1 teaspoon of salt, and stir to combine. Add the tomato paste and cook, stirring occasionally, for about 5 minutes, until the meat is cooked through. Stir in the beef broth and tomatoes. Bring to a boil, then reduce the heat to medium-low, and simmer, stirring occasionally, for 2 hours.

4. Serve the chili hot, garnished with the roasted squash and any other toppings you like.

> TIP   You can often find cubed butternut squash either bagged in the fresh produce section or in the freezer at your local supermarket. If you are starting with a whole squash, microwave it for 6 to 8 minutes before peeling and cutting to make the job easier.

Spicy Chinese Beef in Lettuce Cups

SERVES 4   PREP TIME: 10 MINUTES   COOK TIME: 15 MINUTES

This spicy meat mixture, flavored with garlic, ginger, and coconut aminos, makes a delicious filling for crisp lettuce leaves. For a fun DIY dinner, present the beef in a serving bowl and let people make their own wraps.

2 tablespoons coconut oil

1 small onion, finely diced

1 pound ground beef

2 garlic cloves, minced

2 tablespoons minced peeled fresh ginger

2 tablespoons coconut aminos

1 tablespoon rice vinegar

1 tablespoon sesame oil

1 tablespoons almond butter

2 teaspoons water

2 teaspoons Asian chile paste

1 teaspoon salt

½ cup sliced scallions

½ cup diced water chestnuts

12 lettuce leaves, like Bibb or butter lettuce

¼ cup cashews

1. Heat the coconut oil in a large skillet over medium-high heat. Add the onion and cook, stirring frequently, for about 5 minutes, until softened. Add the beef and cook, stirring and breaking up the meat with a wooden spoon, for about 5 minutes, until browned. Spoon off any excess fat.

2. In a small bowl, whisk together the garlic, ginger, coconut aminos, vinegar, sesame oil, almond butter, water, chile paste, and salt until smooth.

3. Add the mixture to the beef and cook, stirring, for 3 to 4 minutes, until heated through. Stir in the scallions and water chestnuts, and cook until heated through, about 2 minutes more.

4. Serve scooped into lettuce leaves and garnished with cashews.

Classic Beef Stew

SERVES 8   PREP TIME: 15 MINUTES   COOK TIME: 2 HOURS

● ◎ ●   *A classic beef stew is always welcome on a cold evening. Loaded with veggies—carrots, celery, peas, and tomatoes—this one makes a scrumptious one-pot meal. A final touch of fresh parsley elevates the dish with bright, herbaceous notes.*

2 tablespoons coconut oil

1 onion, chopped

2½ pounds beef stew meat, trimmed and cut into 1-inch chunks

¼ cup almond flour

1 garlic clove, minced

1½ teaspoons salt

¾ teaspoon freshly ground black pepper

2 medium carrots, sliced

2 stalks celery, sliced

1 (15-ounce) can diced tomatoes with their juice

2 cups beef broth

2 tablespoons minced flat-leaf parsley

2 teaspoons fresh lemon zest

1. Heat the coconut oil in a large stockpot or Dutch oven over medium-high heat. Add the onion and cook, stirring, for about 5 minutes, until it begins to soften.

2. Season the beef with the salt and pepper. Add the almond flour to a shallow bowl, and dredge the beef in the almond flour. Add the beef to the pan with the garlic, salt, and pepper, and cook, stirring occasionally, for about 4 minutes, until the beef is nicely browned on all sides. ▶

3. Add the carrots, celery, tomatoes, and beef broth, and bring to a boil. Reduce the heat to medium, and cook, stirring occasionally, for 1½ to 2 hours, until the beef is tender and the sauce has thickened.

4. Serve immediately, garnished with parsley and lemon zest.

TIP   Stew is one of those dishes that just gets better and better in the day or two after it was made, so make a big batch you can enjoy more than once. Store the stew in the refrigerator for up to 3 days, or in the freezer for up to 3 months.

Thai Beef and Basil Stir-Fry with Carrot Salad

SERVES 4   PREP TIME: 5 MINUTES   COOK TIME: 15 MINUTES

● ● ●   *This tasty stir-fry of ground beef and fragrant basil is spiked with hot chiles and served with a refreshing and crunchy carrot salad. Best of all, it can be on the table in a mere 20 minutes. To round out the meal, serve with Cauliflower "Rice" (page 372).*

1 tablespoon coconut oil

1 medium onion, thinly sliced

6 garlic cloves, thinly sliced

2 red chiles, thinly sliced

1 teaspoon salt

½ teaspoon freshly ground black pepper

1½ pounds ground beef

½ cup chicken broth

2 cups fresh basil leaves, plus 1 cup

2 cups julienned carrots

1 tablespoon freshly squeezed lime juice, plus 3 tablespoons

1 tablespoon olive oil

2 tablespoons coconut aminos

½ tablespoon fish sauce

1. Heat the coconut oil in a large skillet over medium-high heat. Add the onion and cook, stirring frequently, for about 5 minutes, until softened. Add the garlic, one-half of the sliced chiles, salt, and pepper, and cook, stirring, for about 30 seconds, until fragrant.

2. Add the beef and cook, breaking up the meat with a wooden spoon and stirring occasionally, for about 8 minutes, until the meat is thoroughly browned and cooked through. Stir in the chicken broth and 2 cups of the basil, and cook for 2 minutes, until the basil is wilted. ▶

3. Meanwhile, toss together the carrots, 1 tablespoon of the lime juice, the remaining half of the sliced chiles, the remaining 1 cup basil, and the olive oil in a medium bowl.

4. In a small bowl, add the coconut aminos, the remaining 3 table-spoons lime juice, and fish sauce, and whisk to combine.

5. Serve the beef mixture topped with some of the carrot salad and a drizzle of the coconut aminos sauce.

Bacon-Wrapped Meatloaf

SERVES 4 TO 6   PREP TIME: I5 MINUTES   COOK TIME: 55 MINUTES

A home-style classic, meatloaf is comfort food at its best. This recipe combines beef and pork for great taste and texture. It's then wrapped with bacon strips, creating a crisp outer crust that helps to keep the meatloaf moist while adding delicious, smoky flavor.

1 pound ground beef

½ pound ground pork

2 eggs, lightly beaten

½ cup almond meal

¼ cup tomato paste

1 small onion, diced

½ cup roasted red peppers, drained and minced

½ teaspoon ground cumin

½ teaspoon dried oregano

1 teaspoon salt

½ teaspoon freshly ground black pepper

6 strips bacon

1. Preheat the oven to 350°F.

2. In a large bowl, mix all of the ingredients except the bacon strips together with your hands. Be careful not to overwork the mixture or the meatloaf will be dry.

3. Form the mixture into a loaf about 4 inches tall and 4 inches wide in a large baking pan.

4. Arrange the bacon strips over the top so they cover as much of the loaf as possible.

5. Bake for 45 minutes. Heat the broiler to high, and broil the meatloaf for 10 minutes, until the bacon is crisp and browned. ▶

6. Let the meatloaf rest for 5 to 10 minutes before slicing. Serve hot.

7. Store leftovers, tightly wrapped, in the refrigerator for up to 3 days, or in the freezer for up to 3 months.

TIP   If you don't have roasted peppers, you can easily make your own. Seed 1 large red bell pepper and cut it into a few big pieces. Broil the pieces, skin-side up, under the broiler until the skin is blackened. Place the pieces in a bowl, cover with plastic wrap, and let sit for 10 minutes to loosen the skin. Peel off and discard the skin, and proceed with the recipe.

Flank Steak Stuffed with Sun-Dried Tomato and Spinach Pesto

SERVES 4   PREP TIME: I0 MINUTES   COOK TIME: 30 MINUTES

● ● ●   *Flank steak is relatively lean yet full of flavor. Here it is filled with a rich, tangy sun-dried tomato pesto, seared on the stove top, and finished in the oven. Serve this steak with grilled or roasted vegetables, or a crisp green salad for a simple, yet elegant meal.*

¼ cup sun-dried tomatoes, drained and chopped

1 cup packed baby spinach

1 garlic clove, chopped

2 tablespoons pine nuts

Zest of 1 lemon

Juice of ½ lemon

2 tablespoons olive oil, plus 1 tablespoon

1½ pounds flank steak

¾ teaspoon salt

¼ teaspoon freshly ground black pepper

1. Preheat the oven to 350°F.

2. To make the pesto, add the sun-dried tomatoes, spinach, garlic, pine nuts, lemon zest, and lemon juice in a food processor or blender, and process until finely minced. With the processor running, drizzle in 2 tablespoons of the olive oil until well combined.

3. Place the steak on the work surface, and cover with a sheet of plastic wrap. Using a mallet, pound the meat until it is about ¼ inch thick. Season with the salt and pepper on both sides.

4. Spoon the pesto mixture onto one side of the steak, and spread it evenly with a rubber spatula. Leave about ½ inch clear around the edge of the steak. Roll the steak up and secure it tightly with kitchen twine. ▶

5. Heat the remaining 1 tablespoon olive oil in a skillet over medium-high heat. Add the steak and cook for about 2 minutes on all the sides, until browned. Transfer the skillet to the oven, and bake to desired doneness, about 20 minutes for medium rare or 25 minutes for medium.

6. When the stuffed steak is cooked to your liking, remove it from the oven and let rest for 5 minutes. Slice it into ¼-inch-thick rounds and serve immediately.

TIP   If you've got a batch of Fresh Basil Pesto (page 365), or even a store-bought pesto, feel free to substitute it for the pesto in this recipe (you can even blend in ¼ cup of sun-dried tomatoes if you like). You'll save significant time and effort, and the end result will still be delicious.

Lemon-Rosemary Seared Steak with Asparagus and Mushrooms

SERVES 4   PREP TIME: 10 MINUTES   COOK TIME: 15 MINUTES

● ● ● *It doesn't get much simpler—or more elegant—than seared steak with sautéed asparagus and mushrooms. The refined flavors of lemon zest, rosemary, and garlic make this dish shine.*

1½ pounds 1-inch-thick flank steak

4 garlic cloves, minced

1 tablespoon minced fresh rosemary leaves

½ teaspoon salt, plus ½ teaspoon

¼ teaspoon freshly ground black pepper

1 tablespoon olive oil, plus 1 tablespoon

1 small onion, thinly sliced lengthwise

1 pound asparagus, trimmed and cut into 2-inch pieces

1 pound button or cremini mushrooms, sliced

1 teaspoon grated fresh lemon zest

1. Using a sharp knife, make ⅛-inch-deep cuts in the steak in a crisscross pattern on both sides. Spread half of the garlic and half of the rosemary on both sides of the steak and then sprinkle both sides with ½ teaspoon salt and ¼ teaspoon pepper.

2. Heat 1 tablespoon of the olive oil in a large skillet over medium-high heat. When the pan is very hot, add the steak and cook for about 4 minutes per side for medium rare (add an additional 1 to 2 minutes per side if you prefer it more well done). Transfer the steak to a cutting board, tent with foil, and let rest for at least 5 minutes. ▶

3. Heat the remaining 1 tablespoon olive oil in the skillet and add the onion. Cook, stirring frequently, for about 5 minutes, until the onion begins to soften. Add the remaining garlic and cook for another 1 to 2 minutes. Stir in the asparagus, mushrooms, and the remaining ½ teaspoon of salt, and cook, stirring frequently, for about 5 minutes, until the mushrooms are soft and the asparagus is crisp-tender. Add the lemon zest and the remaining rosemary and stir to combine.

4. To serve, slice the steak across the grain into ¼-inch-thick slices and serve hot with the vegetables.

Lemon-Herb Lamb Skewers

SERVES 8
PREP TIME: 20 MINUTES (PLUS 2 HOURS OR MORE FOR MARINATING)
COOK TIME: 10 MINUTES

● ● ●   *Full of the flavors of Greece, these delicious lamb kabobs make a great party dish for your next backyard barbecue. Just toss together a quick salad and dress it with a red wine vinaigrette to round out the meal. For these kabobs, you'll need about a dozen wooden skewers.*

FOR THE MARINADE

½ cup olive oil

¼ cup freshly squeezed lemon juice

6 garlic cloves, minced

1 white onion, finely chopped

¼ cup chopped fresh mint

2 tablespoons chopped fresh oregano

2 teaspoons chopped fresh rosemary

FOR THE LAMB SKEWERS

4 pounds boneless leg of lamb, trimmed and cut
    into 2-inch cubes

2 large white onions, cut into 2-inch squares

1 green bell pepper, seeded and cut into 2-inch squares

1 orange bell pepper, seeded and cut into 2-inch squares

1 red bell pepper, seeded and cut into 2-inch squares

1 yellow bell pepper, seeded and cut into 2-inch squares

1 pint cherry tomatoes, stemmed

1 (8-ounce) package white button mushrooms

1. To make the marinade, add together all of the marinade ingredients in a large resealable plastic bag or a large bowl. Add the lamb and toss to coat. Seal the bag and refrigerate for at least 2 hours or as long as overnight. ▶

2. To make the lamb skewers, bring the lamb to room temperature by setting it on the countertop for about 30 minutes. At the same time, soak 10 to 12 bamboo skewers in water, and preheat the grill to medium heat.

3. To assemble the lamb skewers, alternate chunks of lamb with slices of onions, peppers, and tomatoes, and whole mushrooms, until all the ingredients have been used up.

4. Cook the skewers on the grill, turning occasionally, for 7 to 8 minutes for medium rare, until charred on all sides. Add 1 to 2 minutes if you want the lamb to be more well done. Serve hot.

Lamb-Stuffed Zucchini
with Fresh Mint

SERVES 4   PREP TIME: I0 MINUTES   COOK TIME: 50 MINUTES

A savory lamb and tomato sauce mixture turns zucchini boats into a scrumptious edible bowl. With fresh mint and a crunchy almond meal topping, this simple dish makes a satisfying, healthful, and speedy meal.

4 medium zucchini, trimmed and halved lengthwise

¼ cup olive oil

1 medium onion, finely chopped

4 garlic cloves, thinly sliced

1 pound ground lamb

2 eggs, lightly beaten

1 bunch fresh mint leaves, stems removed

1 cup Spicy Tomato Sauce (page 368)

1 teaspoon salt, plus more for the zucchini boats

½ teaspoon freshly ground black pepper, plus more
for the zucchini boats

½ cup almond meal

1. Preheat the oven to 450°F.

2. Make a canal down the center of each zucchini half by scooping out the seeds and some of the flesh with a teaspoon. Be sure to leave about ¼ inch of the flesh intact all the way around. Chop the removed zucchini flesh and place in a small bowl.

3. Heat the olive oil in a large skillet over medium-high heat. Add the onion and garlic and cook, stirring frequently, for about 5 minutes, until softened. Add the lamb and cook, stirring and breaking up the meat with a wooden spoon, for about 10 minutes, until the lamb is cooked through. Drain the excess fat and transfer the mixture to a large bowl.

4. Add the eggs, half of the mint leaves, and the tomato sauce to the lamb mixture, and mix well. Season the zucchini boats with pinches of salt and pepper, and add the remaining 1 teaspoon salt and ½ teaspoon pepper to the lamb mixture, and mix well.

5. Fill the zucchini boats with the lamb mixture, piling the filling high. Place the filled boats in a baking dish just large enough to contain them. Sprinkle with the almond meal.

6. Bake the zucchini boats for 20 to 25 minutes, until browned on top.

7. Serve hot, warm, or at room temperature, garnished with the remaining mint leaves.

Lamb Chops with Minted Pea Purée

SERVES 4   PREP TIME: I0 MINUTES   COOK TIME: 20 MINUTES

● ● ●   *Both peas and lamb symbolize the onset of spring, making them a perfect match. Spiking the purée with fresh mint makes it heavenly in its own right and even more complementary with the rich lamb.*

- 1 tablespoon olive oil, plus 1 tablespoon
- 3 garlic cloves, minced
- 2 cups frozen peas (about 12 ounces), thawed
- ¾ cup water, plus more as needed
- ½ teaspoon salt, plus ¼ teaspoon
- ½ teaspoon freshly ground black pepper
- 8 lamb loin chops (1½ to 2 pounds total), trimmed
- 1 tablespoon chopped fresh mint

1. Preheat the oven to 375°F.

2. Heat 1 tablespoon of olive oil in a medium saucepan over medium-high heat. Add the garlic and cook, stirring constantly, for 1 minute. Add the peas, water, and ¼ teaspoon of salt, and bring to a boil. Lower the heat to low, cover, and simmer for 5 minutes. Remove the pan from the heat.

3. Sprinkle both sides of the lamb chops with the remaining ½ teaspoon salt and the pepper. Heat the remaining 1 tablespoon olive oil over medium-high heat in a large, oven-safe skillet. Add the lamb chops and cook for about 2 minutes on one side, until browned on the bottom. Turn the chops over and transfer the skillet to the oven. Bake for 8 to 10 minutes for medium rare, or 1 to 2 minutes longer if you'd like the chops more well done.

4. Meanwhile, place the pea mixture in a food processor or blender, add the mint, and pulse to a coarse purée. If the mixture is too thick, add a bit of water, 1 tablespoon at a time, to thin it.

5. Spoon some of the pea-mint purée onto each of 4 serving plates, and top with 2 lamb chops per person. Serve immediately.

Lamb Shanks Braised with Balsamic Vinegar

SERVES 4   PREP TIME: 10 MINUTES   COOK TIME: 3 HOURS

● ● ●   *Braised lamb shanks make a hearty meal for a winter's evening. Here the shanks are braised in a garlic-spiked mixture of broth and balsamic vinegar, giving the finished dish a deep, complex flavor with just a hint of sweetness to balance out the richness of the lamb.*

1 tablespoon coconut oil, plus 1 tablespoon

1 large onion, sliced

1 teaspoon salt, plus a pinch of salt

5 garlic cloves, smashed

5 celery stalks, including green tops

1 tablespoon chopped fresh rosemary

¼ cup balsamic vinegar

¼ cup coconut aminos

1 cup beef broth

1 (6-ounce) can tomato paste

4 lamb shanks

½ teaspoon freshly ground black pepper

1 (15-ounce) can chickpeas, drained and rinsed

1. Heat 1 tablespoon of the coconut oil in a large stockpot over medium-high heat. Add the onion and a pinch of salt, and cook, stirring frequently, for 1 minute. Add the garlic and continue to cook for about 4 minutes, until the onions are softened. Add the celery and rosemary, and cook for 3 to 4 minutes. Stir in the vinegar and coconut aminos, and mix well. Reduce the heat to medium-low, and simmer for about 5 minutes. Add the beef broth and tomato paste, and cook for 1 minute.

2. Meanwhile, season the lamb shanks all over with 1 teaspoon salt and the pepper. Heat the remaining 1 tablespoon coconut oil in a large skillet over medium-high heat. Add the shanks and cook for about 5 minutes, turning a bit every minute until browned on all sides.

3. Transfer the shanks to the pot, turning to coat them with the braising liquid. Add the chickpeas. Increase the heat to medium-high, bring the braising liquid to a boil, then reduce the heat to low, cover, and simmer for about 2½ hours, turning the shanks over every once in a while, until the meat is very tender and falling from the bone.

4. Serve the lamb shanks hot in shallow bowls, with the braising liquid drizzled over.

Whipped Coconut Cream

SERVES 8   PREP TIME: 10 MINUTES   COOK TIME: NONE

● ● ●   *Nothing compares to a rich, fluffy dollop of whipped cream to top a dessert or even just a bowl of berries. Thanks to this recipe, you can enjoy a dairy-free version that's just as rich and delicious.*

1 (13½-ounce) can full-fat coconut milk, refrigerated overnight
½ teaspoon vanilla extract

1. Remove the can of coconut milk from the refrigerator and without shaking it or turning it over, open the can. Scoop off the thick cream that has risen to the top (you should have about 1 cup) and place it in a mixing bowl. Save the remaining coconut milk for another use.

2. Using an electric mixer set on high speed, whip the cream for 5 to 7 minutes, until it becomes very fluffy and forms soft peaks. Add the vanilla and beat just to incorporate.

TIP   If you can find coconut cream, substitute 1 cup of it for the can of coconut milk in this recipe.

Berries and Cream Parfaits

MAKES 4 PARFAITS   PREP TIME: 5 MINUTES   COOK TIME: NONE

Nothing says summer like a bowl of fresh berries and whipped cream. Here Whipped Coconut Cream stands in for the standard dairy variety, but the result is equally stunning and delicious.

1½ cups fresh raspberries, divided
Whipped Coconut Cream (page 338)
½ cup fresh blackberries
¼ cup unsweetened shredded coconut, for garnish

1. In a medium bowl, gently mash 1 cup of the raspberries. Add half of the whipped coconut cream, and gently stir to mix.

2. In parfait glasses or other glass dessert containers, layer the raspberry-cream mixture, the remaining raspberries, and the blackberries in alternating layers until all of the ingredients are used up.

3. Garnish with a sprinkling of shredded coconut, and serve immediately.

Vanilla Blueberry Coconut Cream Ice Pops

SERVES 6   PREP TIME: 5 MINUTES (PLUS OVERNIGHT TO FREEZE)   COOK TIME: NONE

● ● ●   *A cool, refreshing ice pop is a welcome treat on a hot day. This version gets its beautiful bright purple hue from blueberries. For variety, you can also use blackberries, strawberries, raspberries, or a combination.*

1 (13½-ounce) can coconut milk
½ cup fresh or frozen blueberries
1 teaspoon vanilla extract

1. In a blender, add the coconut milk, blueberries, and vanilla, and process until smooth.

2. Fill 6 (3-ounce) ice pop molds with the mixture, and freeze overnight. Serve frozen.

Crisp Ginger Cookies

MAKES ABOUT 12 COOKIES   PREP TIME: 10 MINUTES   COOK TIME: 15 MINUTES

Face it—sometimes you just need a cookie. These crunchy, spicy ginger cookies are just the thing. Serve them with a cold glass of almond milk for dunking and you've got the perfect after-school snack. If you like, add ¼ cup of chopped nuts along with the unsweetened shredded coconut.

1 small, barely ripe banana, mashed
2 eggs
2 teaspoons coconut oil, melted
½ teaspoon vanilla extract
1 cup unsweetened shredded coconut
1 tablespoon coconut flour
1 teaspoon ground ginger
Pinch of salt

1. Preheat the oven to 350°F. Line a large baking sheet with parchment paper.

2. In a medium bowl, add the mashed banana, eggs, coconut oil, and vanilla, and whisk to combine. Add the shredded coconut, coconut flour, ginger, and salt, and stir to mix well.

3. Drop the cookie dough by heaping spoonfuls onto the prepared baking sheet. Flatten the cookies with the back of a fork.

4. Bake for about 15 minutes, until nicely browned. Transfer to a wire rack to cool. Serve warm or at room temperature.

TIP   Change the flavor of these cookies by using a teaspoon of ground cinnamon in place of the ginger.

Meyer Lemon Pudding

SERVES 4   PREP TIME: 5 MINUTES (PLUS 2 HOURS TO CHILL)   COOK TIME: NONE

This pudding is delightfully simple to make, consisting of just four ingredients. The chia seeds soak up the liquid and form a thick gel that gives the dish its pudding-like consistency, while naturally sweet Meyer lemons provide its irresistible citrus flavor.

1 (13½-ounce) can coconut milk
½ cup chia seeds
¼ teaspoon fresh Meyer lemon zest
Juice of 1 Meyer lemon

1. In a medium mixing bowl, add the coconut milk, chia seeds, lemon zest, and lemon juice, and whisk together until thoroughly blended

2. Ladle the mixture into 4 (4-ounce) ramekins or custard cups, divided equally. Refrigerate for at least 2 hours, until completely set. Serve chilled.

> TIP   If you don't have Meyer lemons, regular lemons—or even limes—will work as well, but the resulting pudding will be less sweet, more tart.

Cinnamon-Spiced Applesauce

_____

SERVES 8   PREP TIME: 5 MINUTES   COOK TIME: 20 MINUTES

Made with nothing but apples, butter, and a dash of cinnamon, this applesauce makes a delicious mid-afternoon snack, after-dinner treat, or even an accompaniment to grilled pork chops or roast pork.

8 green apples, cored, peeled, and diced
4 tablespoons unsalted butter
1 teaspoon cinnamon

1. In a stockpot or large saucepan, add the apples and butter, stir, and heat over medium heat. Cook, stirring frequently, for about 20 minutes, until the apples are very soft.

2. Stir in the cinnamon, and mash the apples to a smooth or chunky consistency.

3. Serve warm, cold, or at room temperature.

> TIP   To make this blue plan–friendly, substitute coconut oil for the butter. But keep in mind that doing so will cause the sauce to solidify when chilled, so you may need to warm it up a bit before serving.

Apple Pecan Crisp

SERVES 4   PREP TIME: 5 MINUTES   COOK TIME: 25 MINUTES

Crisp green apples are sautéed in butter, then baked with a crunchy topping of pecans and spices, for a result resembling apple pie but without all the sugar and flour. Serve this crisp with a dollop of dairy-free Whipped Coconut Cream for an extra special treat.

2 tablespoons unsalted butter, plus 2 tablespoons
3 green apples, cored, peeled, and thinly sliced
½ cup chopped pecans
2 teaspoons ground cinnamon
½ teaspoon ground nutmeg
½ teaspoon salt
Whipped Coconut Cream (page 338), for serving (optional)

1. Preheat the oven to 350°F.

2. Melt 2 tablespoons of the butter in a medium skillet over medium heat. When the butter is foamy, add the apples and cook, stirring occasionally, for about 5 minutes, until the apples are golden brown. Transfer to an 8-inch square baking dish.

3. In a food processor or blender, add the pecans, cinnamon, nutmeg, salt, and the remaining 2 tablespoons butter, and pulse until the mixture resembles a coarse meal. Sprinkle the mixture evenly over the apples, and bake for about 20 minutes, until bubbly and golden brown on top.

4. Serve hot, with a dollop of Whipped Coconut Cream, if desired.

Apple Coconut Bites

MAKES 9 BITES
PREP TIME: 5 MINUTES (PLUS 20 MINUTES TO CHILL)
COOK TIME: 5 MINUTES

● ● ● *Tart green apples are among the few fruits allowed on the sugar detox diet. Here they are cooked and combined with rich coconut cream (also called coconut butter) and a punch of cinnamon for a treat that will satisfy your sweet tooth with very few carbohydrates. Silicone muffin liners are ideal for this recipe, but paper liners will work as well.*

2 tablespoons coconut oil, plus 3 tablespoons

1 green apple, cored, peeled, and diced

2 teaspoons ground cinnamon

Pinch of salt

½ cup coconut cream concentrate or coconut butter

1. Heat 2 tablespoons of the coconut oil in a medium skillet over medium-high heat. Add the apples and cook, stirring occasionally, for about 5 minutes, until softened. Stir in the cinnamon and salt.

2. Put the coconut cream concentrate and the remaining 3 table-spoons coconut oil in a medium microwave-safe bowl, and heat for about 30 seconds to soften. Stir in the cooked apples.

3. Scoop the mixture into 9 silicone or paper muffin liners, dividing equally.

4. Refrigerate for at least 20 minutes to set. Serve chilled.

> **TIP** Coconut cream concentrate, which is sometimes referred to as coconut butter, is concentrated coconut fat made by grinding high-fat coconut meat very finely until it takes on a creamy consistency. It is made up of 70 percent fat, making it is a rich source of pure coconut oil, but it is not suitable for use as a cooking oil.

Coconut Snowball Truffles

MAKES ABOUT 20 TRUFFLES
PREP TIME: 15 MINUTES (PLUS 1 HOUR TO CHILL)
COOK TIME: NONE

● ● ● *These pretty little candies make a lovely offering on a dessert table or a satisfying treat when you need a quick pick-me-up over a long afternoon. Get creative, if you like, and roll the truffles in a variety of coatings, such as chopped nuts, cocoa powder, or crushed cacao nibs.*

1 cup coconut butter
¾ cup coconut oil, at room temperature
½ cup coconut milk
½ cup unsweetened shredded coconut, plus ½ cup
1 tablespoon vanilla extract
⅛ teaspoon salt

1. Add the coconut butter and coconut oil to the bowl of a food processor or blender and process together until smooth. With the processor running, add the coconut milk, ½ cup of the shredded coconut, vanilla, and salt, and process until well combined. Transfer the mixture to a bowl, and refrigerate for 1 hour.

2. Scoop out enough of the mixture to form a 1-inch ball. Roll gently between your palms to make a smooth ball, and place it on a platter. Repeat with the remaining batter until all of the truffles have been formed.

3. Place the remaining ½ cup shredded coconut in a small dish, and roll each ball in the coconut to coat well. Transfer the truffles to a platter as they are completed.

4. Refrigerate at least 1 hour until ready to serve. Serve chilled.

Cocoa Pumpkin Fudge

SERVES 8

PREP TIME: 5 MINUTES (PLUS 4 HOURS TO CHILL)

COOK TIME: NONE

Completely sugar free, this fudge is nonetheless creamy and full of luxurious, chocolaty flavor. It makes a great after-dinner treat, as well as a satisfying afternoon pick-me-up.

1 cup coconut butter, melted

½ cup sunflower seed butter

1 cup pumpkin purée

¼ cup unsweetened cocoa powder, plus additional, for garnish

3 tablespoons coconut oil

½ teaspoon vanilla extract

1. Line an 8-inch square baking dish with parchment paper.

2. Add all of the ingredients in a food processor or blender, and process until well combined and smooth.

3. Transfer the mixture to the prepared baking dish, spread it out evenly, and refrigerate for at least 4 hours to set. Cut into small squares, and serve chilled, with additional cocoa powder sprinkled over the top.

Chocolate Mousse

SERVES 8
PREP TIME: 5 MINUTES (PLUS I HOUR TO CHILL)
COOK TIME: 5 MINUTES

Pumpkin purée and chia seeds are the secret ingredients that give this creamy, chocolaty mousse its custardy thickness and velvety mouthfeel. For an extra-special presentation, serve with a dollop of Whipped Coconut Cream (page 338) and a few curls of dark, unsweetened chocolate on top.

1 (13½-ounce) can coconut milk

¼ cup unsweetened cocoa powder

1 teaspoon ground cinnamon

1 tablespoon vanilla extract

2 tablespoons chia seeds

1 (15-ounce) can puréed pumpkin

1. In a medium saucepan over medium heat, bring the coconut milk to a simmer (do not boil). Add the cocoa powder, cinnamon, and vanilla, and cook, whisking, until very smooth. Remove from the heat and let cool.

2. Meanwhile, place the chia seeds in a food processor or blender and process to a fine powder. Add the cooled coconut milk mixture and the puréed pumpkin to the processor with the chia seeds, and process until smooth. Transfer the mixture to 8 (6-ounce) custard cups or ramekins and chill until completely set, at least 1 hour. Serve chilled.

> **TIP**   Chocolate curls make a delicious, fancy garnish. To make them, soften a hunk of chocolate by microwaving it at 50 percent power for just about 30 seconds. Then use a vegetable peeler to shave off curls by scraping the blade lengthwise across the chocolate. Keep the curls refrigerated until ready to use. Easy!

Banana Chocolate Shake

SERVES 1   PREP TIME: 5 MINUTES   COOK TIME: NONE

● ● ●   *An icy-cold shake is the perfect treat for a hot summer day. This one combines banana, protein-rich almond butter, coconut milk, and chocolaty cocoa powder. Vanilla extract and cinnamon round out the flavors making the addition of any form of sweetener wholly unnecessary.*

1 barely ripe banana
¾ cup coconut milk
2 tablespoons almond butter
1 tablespoon gelatin
1 tablespoon unsweetened cocoa powder
½ teaspoon vanilla extract
¼ teaspoon cinnamon

Place all of the ingredients in a blender, and first blend on medium speed for 1 to 2 minutes, then on high speed for 1 minute, until smooth. Serve immediately.

Banana Chocolate Almond Ice Cream

SERVES 4   PREP TIME: 5 MINUTES   COOK TIME: NONE

Bananas, chocolate, and almond butter make a richly satisfying dairy-free (and sugar-free) ice cream. Serve it immediately, and it will be the texture of soft-serve. For a more ice cream–like consistency, freeze it for 4 hours, stirring occasionally, before serving.

4 cups sliced frozen bananas

1 cup coconut milk or almond milk

¼ cup almond butter

2 teaspoons unsweetened cocoa powder

½ teaspoon vanilla extract

1. In a food processor or blender, add the bananas and coconut milk, and process until smooth.

2. Add the almond butter, cocoa powder, and vanilla. Blend to mix well. Serve immediately.

TIP   For variety, you can substitute peanut butter (if you're on the yellow plan) or hazelnut butter for the almond butter.

Coconut-Filled Chocolates

SERVES 9

PREP TIME: 10 MINUTES (PLUS 60 MINUTES TO CHILL)

COOK TIME: 10 MINUTES

These decadent dark chocolates filled with a mixture of coconut milk and unsweetened shredded coconut are like a super nutritious version of a Mounds candy bar. The chocolate shell is prepared in two stages and chilled in between. Make these candies using a silicone candy mold or silicone mini-muffin liners, if you can. Otherwise, mini-muffin paper liners will work.

¼ cup coconut milk

5 tablespoons unsweetened shredded coconut

1 teaspoon vanilla extract

2 tablespoons coconut oil, plus 2 tablespoons

2½ tablespoons unsweetened cocoa powder, plus 2½ tablespoons

Salt

1. In a small saucepan, add the coconut milk and shredded coconut, and cook over low heat, stirring occasionally, for 5 minutes. Remove from the heat and stir in the vanilla. Let cool for 5 minutes, then refrigerate.

2. Meanwhile, in a separate small saucepan, warm 2 tablespoons of the coconut oil over medium heat. Add 2½ tablespoons of the cocoa powder and a pinch of salt, and cook, stirring, until well combined and smooth.

3. Pour the cocoa mixture into 9 silicone candy molds, dividing equally. Refrigerate for 30 minutes.

4. Remove both the filling mixture and the chocolate shells from the refrigerator. Place a dollop of the filling into the center of each chocolate shell, using about 1 teaspoon of filling per chocolate. ▶

5. To prepare the remaining cocoa mixture, warm the remaining 2 tablespoons coconut oil over medium heat. Add the remaining 2½ tablespoons cocoa powder and a pinch of salt and cook, stirring, until well combined and smooth.

6. Pour the mixture into the molds, covering the filling. Refrigerate for at least 30 minutes longer or until ready to serve. Serve the chocolates chilled.

Hot Chocolate with Coconut Milk

SERVES 4   PREP TIME: 5 MINUTES   COOK TIME: 5 MINUTES

● ● ●   *A cup of rich hot chocolate can warm both body and soul. Coconut milk adds a tropical touch, and the bitterness of the chocolate is mellowed by a dash of vanilla extract. Even without any added sugar, this warming drink satisfies any cravings for the sweet stuff.*

1½ cups coconut milk
1½ cups water
½ cup plus 1 tablespoon unsweetened cocoa powder
½ teaspoon vanilla extract
Cinnamon, for garnish (optional)

1. Put all of the ingredients in a medium saucepan and whisk to combine.

2. Heat over medium heat until simmering, and cook for about 5 minutes.

3. Serve hot, garnished with a sprinkling of cinnamon, if desired.

FIFTEEN

KITCHEN BASICS

Balsamic Vinaigrette

MAKES ABOUT I CUP (ABOUT 8 [2-TABLESPOON] SERVINGS)
PREP TIME: 3 MINUTES
COOK TIME: NONE

● ● ●   *Bottled salad dressings—even the so-called healthy ones—are often loaded with sugar. This simple sweet-tart vinaigrette takes just a few minutes to make and contains only healthful ingredients that are likely in your pantry already. Best of all, you can use it to dress just about any salad combination.*

¼ cup balsamic vinegar

2 tablespoons Dijon mustard

1½ teaspoons salt

¾ teaspoon freshly ground black pepper

6 tablespoons olive oil

1. In a small bowl, whisk together the vinegar, mustard, salt, and pepper. Add the olive oil, and whisk until the dressing is emulsified.

2. The vinaigrette can be stored in the refrigerator in an airtight jar for up to 2 weeks, but bring it to room temperature and shake well before using.

Tahini Lemon Dressing

MAKES ABOUT ½ CUP (ABOUT 4 [2-TABLESPOON] SERVINGS)
PREP TIME: 5 MINUTES
COOK TIME: NONE

● ● ●   *Tahini is a paste made from ground sesame seeds. It provides a nutty flavor and a rich, creamy consistency to salad dressings and sauces. This simple dressing is a wonderfult all-purpose condiment. You can drizzle it over steamed broccoli or asparagus, sautéed greens, or salad greens, or use it as a dip for steamed artichoke leaves.*

3 tablespoons freshly squeezed lemon juice

2 tablespoons water

2 tablespoons tahini

1 small clove garlic, minced

½ teaspoon salt

⅛ teaspoon cayenne pepper

In a small bowl, whisk all of the ingredients together until smooth. Store in an airtight jar in the refrigerator for up to 1 week.

Pico de Gallo

MAKES ABOUT 2½ CUPS (ABOUT 4 SERVINGS)
PREP TIME: 10 MINUTES
COOK TIME: NONE

● ● ●   *An outstanding pico de gallo (also called "salsa fresca," or fresh salsa) is fresh and bright, with a touch of heat and the herbaceous bite of fresh cilantro. Delicious as a dip for veggie sticks, it can equally be used as a sauce for grilled fish or chicken, spooned over eggs, or spicing up a lettuce-wrap taco.*

½ cup finely diced red onion
1 garlic clove, minced
Juice of 1 lime
½ teaspoon salt, plus more if needed
1 to 2 jalapeño chile peppers, seeded and diced
4 to 6 plum tomatoes, diced
½ cup chopped fresh cilantro

1. Place the onion and garlic in a small bowl, and squeeze the lime juice over the them. Add the salt and let the mixture rest for a few minutes to soften the onions and meld the flavors.

2. Stir in 1 jalapeño chile, the tomatoes, and cilantro. Taste and add more salt or more jalapeño, if needed.

3. Cover and refrigerate for 1 to 2 hours to let the flavors meld. Serve immediately or store in the refrigerator for up to 3 days.

Homemade Mayonnaise

MAKES ABOUT ¾ CUP (ABOUT 12 [1-TABLESPOON] SERVINGS)
PREP TIME: 5 MINUTES
COOK TIME: NONE

Once you've tried homemade mayonnaise, you'll never want to go back to the store-bought stuff—and not just because it's usually loaded with hidden sugar. Homemade mayonnaise just tastes so much better. This classic version is made with egg yolk and olive oil, and just a bit of lemon juice, vinegar, Dijon mustard, and salt for flavor.

1 large egg yolk

1½ teaspoons freshly squeezed lemon juice

1 teaspoon white wine vinegar

¼ teaspoon Dijon mustard

½ teaspoon salt

¾ cup olive oil

1. In a blender or food processor, blend together the egg yolk, lemon juice, vinegar, mustard, and salt. With the blender or processor running, drizzle the olive oil in slowly. Continue processing until all of the oil has been added and the mixture is thick.

2. Transfer to an airtight jar and store in the refrigerator for up to 3 days.

> **TIP** If your homemade mayonnaise breaks or curdles (the mixture loses its emulsification and the fats and solids separate), you can easily fix it by adding another egg yolk or a bit of hot water. To use an additional egg yolk, whisk the yolk and then slowly add it to the curdled mayonnaise, whisking constantly, until the mixture is thick and smooth. To use hot water, slowly drizzle about 1 tablespoon of very hot water into the curdled mayonnaise, whisking constantly, until smooth.

Fresh Basil Pesto

MAKES ABOUT 1 CUP (8 [2-TABLESPOON] SERVINGS)
PREP TIME: 5 MINUTES
COOK TIME: NONE

Simple, flavorful, and classic, a good fresh basil pesto can be used in so many ways beyond saucing grain flour–laden pasta. Try stirring it into salad dressings, mixing it into meatballs or meatloaf, spreading it on wraps, or blending it with puréed beans into a flavorful spread. This version uses nutritional yeast—which can be found in any health food store or natural foods store—in place of the traditional Parmesan cheese.

3 cloves garlic
⅓ cup walnuts
2 cups fresh basil leaves
2 tablespoons nutritional yeast
½ cup olive oil
Salt
Freshly ground black pepper

1. Chop the garlic in a food processor or blender. Add the walnuts and pulse to chop. Add the basil and process until finely chopped. Add the nutritional yeast, and pulse 2 to 3 times to mix.

2. With the food processor running, add the olive oil in a thin stream, stopping to scrape down the sides of the bowl as needed. Season with salt and pepper. Serve immediately, or store in the refrigerator in an airtight jar for up to 1 week, or in the freezer for up to 3 months.

TIP   Just about any fresh herb can be used for pesto. Try replacing the basil with cilantro, mint, or parsley. The walnuts, too, can be replaced with pine nuts, pecans, almonds, or peanuts.

Sugar-Free Ketchup

MAKES ABOUT 1½ CUPS
PREP TIME: 5 MINUTES (PLUS 4 HOURS TO CHILL)
COOK TIME: NONE

Store-bought ketchup is almost always full of sugar, corn syrup, or other sweeteners. Make your own, however, and you'll discover that good ketchup doesn't need sugar. This version is especially easy to prepare since it doesn't require cooking.

2 (6-ounce) cans tomato paste
¼ cup apple cider vinegar
1 tablespoon Dijon mustard
¼ cup plus 2 tablespoons water
½ teaspoon salt
½ teaspoon ground cinnamon
⅛ teaspoon ground cloves
¼ teaspoon garlic powder

1. In a blender, add all of the ingredients, and blend until well combined and smooth.

2. Transfer the ketchup to an airtight jar, and refrigerate for at least 4 hours before serving. Store in the refrigerator for up to 2 weeks.

TIP   If your ketchup is thinner than you'd like, you can thicken it up with chia seeds that have been powdered in a blender or food processor. Add 1 teaspoon chia seed powder, mix well, and refrigerate for several hours.

Spicy Tomato Sauce

MAKES ABOUT 9 CUPS (ABOUT 18 [½-CUP] SERVINGS)
PREP TIME: 10 MINUTES
COOK TIME: 1 HOUR 10 MINUTES

In any supermarket, you'll find dozens of jarred tomato sauces. Many of them are even organic or all-natural, but nearly every one contains some kind of added sweetener. Make a giant batch of your own, and you'll have delicious, no-sugar-added tomato sauce at the ready whenever you need it.

2 tablespoons olive oil

3 medium onions, chopped

4 cloves garlic, minced

2 tablespoons balsamic vinegar

3 (26½-ounce) boxes crushed tomatoes

2 teaspoons dried oregano

1 teaspoon salt

1 teaspoon freshly ground black pepper

1 teaspoon cayenne pepper

1. Heat the olive oil in a large stockpot over medium-high heat.

2. Add the onions, and cook, stirring occasionally, for about 5 minutes, until soft.

3. Add the garlic and continue to cook, stirring, for about 1 minute.

4. Stir in the balsamic vinegar, tomatoes, oregano, salt, pepper, and cayenne pepper.

5. Bring the mixture to a boil, reduce the heat to low, and simmer, uncovered, for about 1 hour, until the sauce is thickened. Let cool. Transfer to glass storage containers, and store in the refrigerator for up to 1 week or in the freezer for up to 3 months.

TIP Canned tomatoes are among the foods most likely to contain BPA (bisphenol-A) leached from the can's plastic lining because of tomatoes' natural acidity. Choose tomatoes packaged in boxes rather than in cans to avoid this risk.

Homemade Almond Milk

MAKES ABOUT 2 CUPS (ABOUT 4 [½-CUP] SERVINGS)
PREP TIME: 10 MINUTES (PLUS OVERNIGHT TO SOAK THE ALMONDS)
COOK TIME: NONE

Store-bought almond milk often contains added sweeteners and other puzzling ingredients, but making your own is easy, and you can control its contents. Just soak the almonds overnight, blend with water, and strain, and you've got all-natural, additive-free almond milk.

1 cup raw almonds
2 cups cold water, plus more for soaking

1. Place the almonds in a medium bowl, and add cold water to cover by about 1 inch. Let the almonds soak, uncovered, overnight.

2. Drain the almonds, discarding the soaking water, put them in a colander, and rinse them thoroughly with cold water.

3. Transfer the almonds to a blender with the 2 cups of water, and process at high speed for 2 minutes. Scrape down the sides of the bowl, if needed, and process for another 2 to 3 minutes, until the nuts are very finely ground and the liquid is white and opaque.

4. Line a colander with a fine-meshed nut-milk bag or a square of cheesecloth, and place it over a bowl. Pour the puréed almond mixture into the nut-milk bag, letting the liquid run into the bowl. Squeeze the bag to get as much liquid out of it as you can. Serve immediately.

5. Almond milk can be stored in the refrigerator in an airtight glass container for up to 2 days.

TIP   The almonds should be soaked for at least 8 to 12 hours, but they can be soaked for as long as 2 days. The longer you soak them, the creamier the resulting almond milk will be.

Cauliflower "Rice"

SERVES 4   PREP TIME: 5 MINUTES   COOK TIME: 5 MINUTES

Cauliflower makes a great substitute for rice and other grains. Its mild flavor is well suited to just about any cuisine, making it a good base for any dish in which you want to capture a sauce or juices. It's also a blank slate that can be seasoned in many different ways—add lemon or lime juice or zest, chopped fresh herbs like cilantro, basil, or mint, or ground spices like cumin or chili powder.

1 large head cauliflower, cut into florets
1 tablespoon olive oil or coconut oil
½ teaspoon salt
¼ teaspoon freshly ground black pepper

1. In the bowl of a food processor, pulse the florets until they are in small rice-sized pieces. You may need to process the cauliflower in multiple batches.

2. Heat the olive oil in a large skillet over medium-high heat. Add the cauliflower and cook, stirring occasionally, about 5 minutes, until it is softened and beginning to brown. Stir in the salt and pepper.

TIP   For the best results, make sure your cauliflower is very dry before you process it.

Cashew Cheese

MAKES ABOUT 1½ CUPS (12 [2-TABLESPOON] SERVINGS)
PREP TIME: 10 MINUTES (PLUS 30 MINUTES TO SOAK THE CASHEWS)
COOK TIME: NONE

Cashew cheese is a rich, creamy, dairy-free cheese substitute. You can substitute cashew cheese in just about anything for which you'd use dairy cheese—drizzle it on enchiladas, grain-free pizza, salads, or wraps.

1 cup cashews

¼ cup water

¼ cup nutritional yeast

2 tablespoons freshly squeezed lemon juice

2 garlic cloves, chopped

2 tablespoons white wine vinegar

1 tablespoon Dijon mustard

¼ teaspoon salt

Put all of the ingredients in a blender, and process until the mixture is smooth and creamy. Serve immediately, or store in an airtight container in the refrigerator for up to 1 week.

> **TIP** Nutritional yeast can be found in any health food or natural foods store, and it provides that difficult-to-pin-down fermented flavor that you expect from cheese.

DAILY NUTRITION GUIDELINES

Food Groups and Serving Sizes per Day or Week

FOOD GROUP	SERVINGS PER DAY OR WEEK
Grains	7 to 8 per day
Vegetables	4 to 5 per day
Fruits	4 to 5 per day
Dairy	2 to 3 per day
Meats, poultry, and fish	2 or fewer per day
Legumes, nuts, and seeds	4 to 5 per week
Sweeteners	5 or fewer per week
Fats and oils	2 to 3 per day

APPENDIX B MEASUREMENT CONVERSIONS

Volume Equivalents (Liquid)

US STANDARD (OUNCES)	US STANDARD (APPROXIMATE)	METRIC
2 tablespoons	1 fl. oz.	30 mL
¼ cup	2 fl. oz.	60 mL
½ cup	4 fl. oz.	120 mL
1 cup	8 fl. oz.	240 mL
1½ cups	12 fl. oz.	355 mL
2 cups or 1 pint	16 fl. oz.	475 mL
4 cups or 1 quart	32 fl. oz.	1 L
1 gallon	128 fl. oz.	4 L

Oven Temperatures

FAHRENHEIT (F)	CELSIUS (C) (APPROXIMATE)
250	120
300	150
325	165
350	180
375	190
400	200
425	220
450	230

Volume Equivalents (Dry)

US STANDARD	METRIC (APPROXIMATE)
⅛ teaspoon	.5 mL
¼ teaspoon	1 mL
½ teaspoon	2 mL
¾ teaspoon	4 mL
1 teaspoon	5 mL
1 tablespoon	15 mL
¼ cup	59 mL
⅓ cup	79 mL
½ cup	118 mL
⅔ cup	156 mL
¾ cup	177 mL
1 cup	235 mL
2 cups or 1 pint	475 mL
3 cups	700 mL
4 cups or 1 quart	1 L
½ gallon	2 L
1 gallon	4 L

Weight Equivalents

US STANDARD	METRIC (APPROXIMATE)
½ ounce	15 g
1 ounce	30 g
2 ounces	60 g
4 ounces	115 g
8 ounces	225 g
12 ounces	340 g
16 ounces or 1 pound	455 g

RESOURCES

Books

Alpert, Brooke, MS, RD. *The Sugar Detox: Lose Weight, Feel Great, and Look Years Younger*. Cambridge, MA: Da Capo Lifelong Books, 2013.

Hyman, Mark, MD. *The Blood Sugar Solution 10-Day Detox Diet: Activate Your Body's Natural Ability to Burn Fat and Lose Weight Fast*. Boston, MA: Little, Brown and Company, 2014.

Sanfilippo, Diane. *The 21-Day Sugar Detox: Bust Sugar & Carb Cravings Naturally*. Las Vegas, NV: Victory Belt Publishing, 2013.

Websites

The 21-Day Sugar Detox   the21daysugardetox.com

Balanced Bites   balancedbites.com/21dsd

Foodee   thefoodee.com/tag/21dsd

Fresh4Five   fresh4five.com

The Gracious Pantry   thegraciouspantry.com

Dr. Mark Hyman   drhyman.com

Primal Palate   primalpalate.com

REFERENCES

Ahmed, SH, K. Guillem, and Y. Vandaele. "Sugar Addiction: Pushing the Drug-Sugar Analogy to the Limit." *Current Opinion in Clinical Nutrition and Metabolic Care* 16, no. 4 (July 2013): 434–9.

American Heart Association. "Frequently Asked Questions About Sugar." Accessed June 6, 2014. http://www.heart.org/HEARTORG /GettingHealthy/NutritionCenter/HealthyEating/Frequently -Asked-Questions-About-Sugar_UCM_306725_Article.jsp

American Heart Association. "Dietary Sugars Intake and Cardiovascular Health." Accessed June 8, 2014. http://circ.ahajournals.org/content /120/11/1011.abstract?searchid=1&HITS=10&hits=10&resourcetype =HWCIT&maxtoshow=&RESULTFORMAT=&FIRSTINDEX=0& fulltext=sugar

Egger, G. "In Search of a Germ Theory Equivalent for Chronic Disease." *Preventing Chronic Disease* (May 2012).

MacPherson, Kitta. "Sugar Can Be Addictive, Princeton Scientist Says." Princeton.edu. Accessed June 6, 2014. http://www.princeton.edu /main/news/archive/S22/88/56G31/index.xml?section=topstories

Purdue.edu. "Prof: Diet Drinks Are Not the Sweet Solution to Fight Obesity, Health Problems." Accessed June 6, 2014. http://www .purdue.edu/newsroom/releases/2013/Q3/prof-diet-drinks-are-not -the-sweet-solution-to-fight-obesity,-health-problems.html

RECIPE INDEX

INDEX

CPSIA information can be obtained at www.ICGtesting.com
Printed in the USA
BVOW11s1054141114

374514BV00001B/1/P

9 780989 558662